KAWAII CROCHET CHRISTMAS

40 super cute amigurumi patterns for the festive season

Melissa Bradley-Vatcher

DAVID & CHARLES
—PUBLISHING—

www.davidandcharles.com

CONTENTS

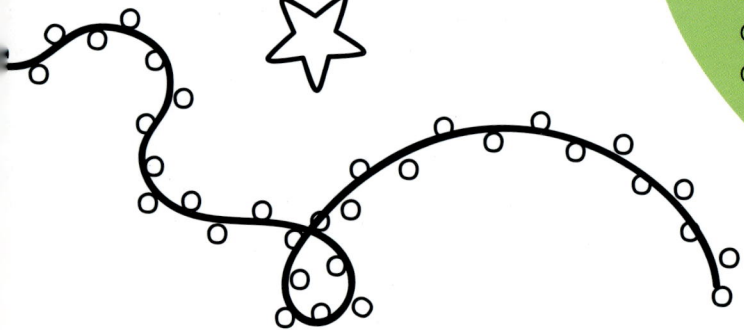

TECHNIQUES

INTRODUCTION

Kawaii Crochet Christmas is the third installment in a series of cute amigurumi books that I have had the privilege to create. Its aim is to spread joy and bring smiles to the faces of readers and makers alike and hopefully bring an added measure of cheer to the holiday season. Filled with adorable festive patterns, this book is perfect for anyone looking to add a touch of charm to their holiday decorations as well as to their handmade gift giving. From a super cute reindeer cake and an appealing penguin to romantic mistletoe, there is something for everyone in this delightful collection.

What's more, each pattern can be easily modified into a festive Christmas ornament or gift embellishment. Simply follow my tips for modifying the size of the design as well as creating a hanging loop and turn each pattern into a hanging ornament for the most delightfully decorated Christmas tree.

Creating this book has brought me so much enjoyment and it is my hope that the patterns on these pages will bring you that joy as well—especially during the holiday season—and allow for the creation of unique and meaningful gifts for your loved ones. May your holiday include the satisfaction of giving your handmade items and seeing the recipients experience an added measure of warmth and joy knowing that they were made with such love and care.

So, let's get ready to create some kawaii magic and make this holiday season extra special with these patterns. I hope we all discover a love for crochet, Christmas, and all things cute!

Wishing you a very merry Christmas and

Happy Crocheting!

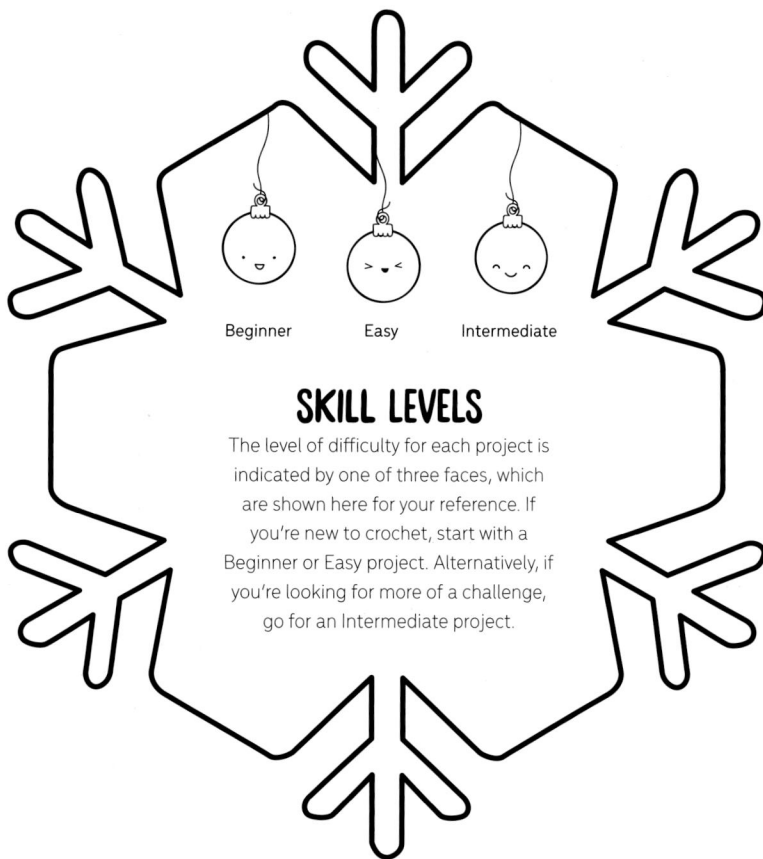

Beginner   Easy   Intermediate

SKILL LEVELS

The level of difficulty for each project is indicated by one of three faces, which are shown here for your reference. If you're new to crochet, start with a Beginner or Easy project. Alternatively, if you're looking for more of a challenge, go for an Intermediate project.

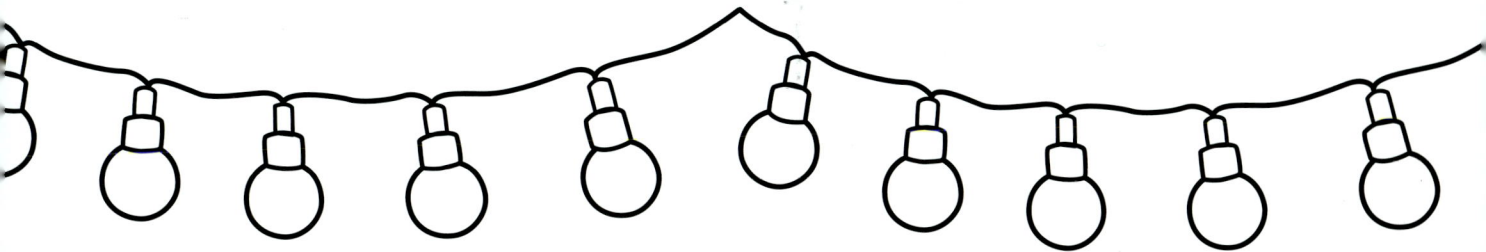

TOOLS AND MATERIALS

STITCH MARKERS

With my stitch marker I always mark the last stitch of the round. Alternatively, use a piece of yarn in a contrast color, a safety pin, or a paper clip.

CROCHET HOOKS

Sizes 2.75mm (US C/2) and 3.5mm (US E/4). My favorites are Clover Amour crochet hooks; they are so comfy!

FIBERFILL STUFFING

Important for getting the right shape for your amigurumi. I use a polyester fiberfill stuffing.

PINS

For keeping parts together. I like to use T-pins so that they don't get lost inside my amigurumi.

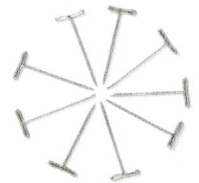

FLORAL WIRE

Green wire, specifically 26-gauge.

HOT GLUE GUN

My secret weapon when making amigurumi. When a pattern says "attach", that is when the hot glue gun gets plugged in! Now, a crochet purist would say...glue, no way! But I have found that when attaching bits and pieces to these kawaii characters, a hot glue gun is much faster and easier in the end. Of course, you can always use a needle and thread instead.

TOY SAFETY EYES

Black, sizes 5mm through 9mm, are what I use the most. Alternatively, use black yarn to embroider eyes (see Making Up: Inserting Safety Eyes).

SCISSORS

One of my favorite things to collect. They are best when they are pointy, sharp, and colorful!

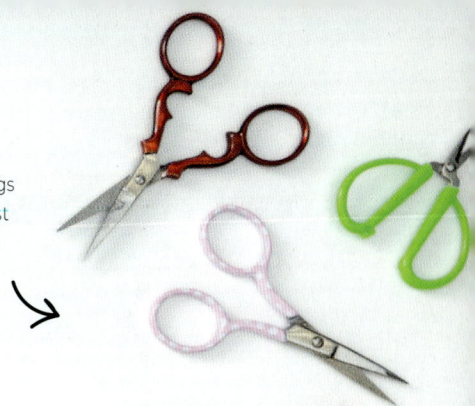

TAPESTRY NEEDLE

Longer and sharper than a yarn needle, a tapestry needle is essential for shaping taller amigurumi like the Christmas candle.

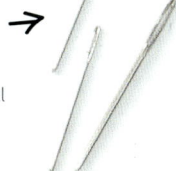

YARN NEEDLE

This is a blunt needle and is essential for weaving in ends and shaping.

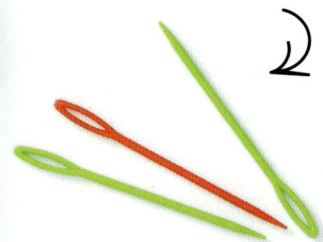

POM-POM MAKER

Optional, you can certainly make a pom-pom without a pom-pom maker, but they make it so much easier. You'll need the extra small size, specifically 2.5cm (1in).

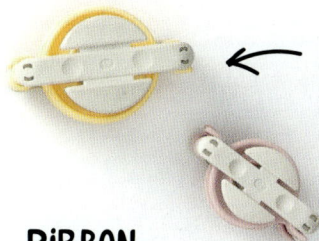

COTTON YARN

Two different yarn weights are used throughout this book and sometimes in the same pattern: Aran (worsted) 4ply and DK (light worsted) 3ply.

RIBBON

Ribbon is essential when it comes to making DIY Christmas gifts that everyone will love.

WIRE CUTTERS

Resist the urge to use your scissors! Your hands (and scissors) will thank you later.

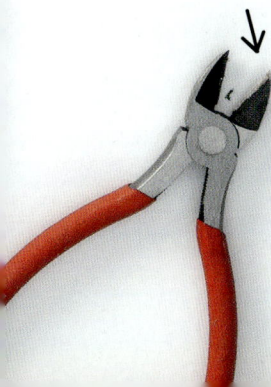

NOVELTY YARN

Specialty yarn that has unique color and/or texture to add visual interest to the fabric.

PROJECTS

CHRISTMAS BAUBLES

BALL SHAPE BAUBLE

Rnd 1: with **gray** yarn, sc 6 in magic loop [6]

Rnd 2: 2 sc in each st around [12]

Rnd 3: working in BLO, sc in each st around [12]

Rnd 4: sc in each st around [12]

Rnd 5: change to **red** yarn, working in BLO, (sc 1, 2 sc in next st) repeat 6 times [18]

Rnd 6: (sc 2, 2 sc in next st) repeat 6 times [24]

Rnd 7: (sc 3, 2 sc in next st) repeat 6 times [30]

Rnd 8: (sc 4, 2 sc in next st) repeat 6 times [36]

Rnd 9: (sc 5, 2 sc in next st) repeat 6 times [42]

Rnds 10–17: sc in each st around [42] 8 rounds

Place 8mm safety eyes between **Rnds 12 and 13** with 5 sts in between. Begin to stuff with fiberfill.

I LIKE HANGING WITH YOU

DROP SHAPE BAUBLE

Rnd 1: with **gray** yarn, sc 6 in magic loop [6]

Rnd 2: 2 sc in each st around [12]

Rnd 3: working in BLO, sc in each st around [12]

Rnd 4: sc in each st around [12]

Rnd 5: change to **red** yarn, working in BLO, (sc 1, 2 sc in next st) repeat 6 times [18]

Rnd 6: sc in each st around [18]

Rnd 7: (sc 2, 2 sc in next st) repeat 6 times [24]

Rnd 8: sc in each st around [24]

Rnd 9: (sc 3, 2 sc in next st) repeat 6 times [30]

Rnd 10: sc in each st around [30]

Rnd 11: (sc 4, 2 sc in next st) repeat 6 times [36]

Rnds 12–16: sc in each st around [36]

Place 8mm safety eyes between **Rnds 13 and 14** with 4 sts in between. Begin to stuff with fiberfill.

Rnd 17: (sc 4, sc2tog) repeat 6 times [30]

Rnd 18: (sc 3, sc2tog) repeat 6 times [24]

Rnd 19: (sc 6, sc2tog) repeat 3 times [21]

Rnd 20: (sc 5, sc2tog) repeat 3 times [18]

Rnd 21: (sc 4, sc2tog) repeat 3 times [15]

Rnd 22: (sc 3, sc2tog) repeat 3 times [12]

Rnd 23: (sc 2, sc2tog) repeat 3 times [9]

Rnd 24: (sc 1, sc2tog) repeat 3 times [6]

Finish stuffing with fiberfill. Fasten off and leave a long yarn tail. With a yarn needle, weave the tail through FLO to close opening. Weave in all ends.

Stitch the mouth and cheeks using **black** and **pink** yarn.

Add a hanging loop using **gray** yarn.

ONION SHAPE BAUBLE

Rnd 1: with **gray** yarn, sc 6 in magic loop [6]

Rnd 2: 2 sc in each st around [12]

Rnd 3: working in BLO, sc in each st around [12]

Rnd 4: sc in each st around [12]

Rnd 5: change to **red** yarn, working in BLO, (sc 1, 2 sc in next st) repeat 6 times [18]

Rnd 6: (sc 2, 2 sc in next st) repeat 6 times [24]

Rnd 7: (sc 3, 2 sc in next st) repeat 6 times [30]

Rnd 8: (sc 4, 2 sc in next st) repeat 6 times [36]

Rnd 9: (sc 5, 2 sc in next st) repeat 6 times [42]

Rnds 10–15: sc in each st around [42] 8 rounds

Place 8mm safety eyes between **Rnds 12 and 13** with 5 sts in between. Begin to stuff with fiberfill.

Rnd 16: (sc 5, sc2tog) repeat 6 times [36]

Rnd 17: (sc 4, sc2tog) repeat 6 times [30]

Rnd 18: (sc 3, sc2tog) repeat 6 times [24]

Rnd 19: (sc 2, sc2tog) repeat 6 times [18]

Rnd 20: (sc 4, sc2tog) repeat 3 times [15]

Rnd 21: (sc 3, sc2tog) repeat 3 times [12]

Rnd 22: (sc 2, sc2tog) repeat 3 times [9]

Rnd 23: (sc 1, sc2tog) repeat 3 times [6]

Finish stuffing with fiberfill. Fasten off and leave a long yarn tail. With yarn needle, weave the tail through FLO to close opening. Weave in all ends.

Stitch the mouth and cheeks using **black** and **pink** yarn.

Add a hanging loop using **gray** yarn.

Rnd 18: (sc 5, sc2tog) repeat 6 times [36]

Rnd 19: (sc 4, sc2tog) repeat 6 times [30]

Rnd 20: (sc 3, sc2tog) repeat 6 times [24]

Rnd 21: (sc 2, sc2tog) repeat 6 times [18]

Rnd 22: (sc 1, sc2tog) repeat 6 times [12]

Rnd 23: (sc2tog) repeat 6 times [6]

Finish stuffing. Fasten off and leave a long yarn tail. With a yarn needle and the tail, weave through FLO to close opening, weave in ends.

Stitch the mouth and cheeks using **black** and **pink** yarn (see Making Up: Stitching Facial Details).

Add a hanging loop using **gray** yarn (see Making Up: Ornament Hanging Loop).

ROBIN

> SEASON'S TWEETINGS!

Materials

- 2.75mm (C/2) crochet hook
- Paintbox Yarns Cotton DK yarn: one 50g (1¾oz) ball each of Soft Fudge (**light brown**), Coffee Bean (**dark brown**), Blood Orange (**orange**), and Pure Black (**black**)
- 6mm safety eyes
- Fiberfill stuffing
- Yarn needle
- Stitch marker

Finished Size

5.5cm (2¼in) tall by 8.5cm (3¼in) wide

Gauge

6 sc sts and 7 rows = 2.5cm (1in)

ROBIN

Rnd 1: with **light brown** yarn sc 6 in magic loop [6]

Rnd 2: 2 sc in each st around [12]

Rnd 3: (sc 1, 2 sc in next st) repeat 6 times [18]

Rnd 4: (sc 2, 2 sc in next st) repeat 6 times [24]

Rnds 5–7: sc in each st around [24]

Rnd 8: 3 sc in next st, sc 23 [26]

Rnd 9: sc 1, 3 sc in next st, sc 24 [28]

Rnd 10: sc 2, 3 sc in next st, sc 12, change to **orange** yarn, sc 3, change to **light brown** yarn, sc 10 [30]

Rnd 11: sc 3, 3 sc in next st, sc 12, change to **orange** yarn, sc 5, change to **light brown** yarn, sc 9 [32]

Rnd 12: sc 4, for the tail, sc 1 + ch 6 + sc in 2nd ch from hook + sc in next 4 ch sts + sc 1 in same st, sc 12, change to **orange** yarn, sc 7, change to **light brown** yarn, sc 8 [38]

Rnd 13: sc 5, sc 5 in lower loops of ch 6 from **Rnd 12**, sc 5 in tail sts, sc 12, change to **orange** yarn, sc 9, change to **light brown** yarn, sc 7 [43]

Rnd 14: sc 2, (2 sc in next st, sc 1) repeat 4 times, (sc 1, 2 sc in next st) repeat 4 times, sc 10, change to **orange** yarn, sc 7, change to **light brown** yarn, sc 8 [51]

Rnd 15: (sc 4, 2 sc in next st) repeat 2 times, sc 8, 2 sc in next st, sc 4, 2 sc in next st, sc 13, change to **orange** yarn, sc 5, change to **light brown** yarn, sc 9 [55]

Rnd 16: sc 42, change to **orange** yarn, sc 3, change to **light brown** yarn sc 10 [55]

Place 6mm safety eyes between **Rnds 6 and 7** with 5 sts in between. Begin to stuff with fiberfill.

Rnd 17: sc 7, skip next 20 sts, sc 28 [35] (1)

Rnd 18: (sc2tog, sc3) repeat 7 times [28]

Rnd 19: (sc2tog) repeat 14 times [14]

Rnd 20: (sc2tog) repeat 7 times [7]

Finish stuffing. Fasten off and leave a long yarn tail. With a yarn needle, weave the tail through FLO to close the opening, weave in ends.

Stuff the tail lightly with fiberfill and sew together (2).

BEAK

Rnd 1: with **black** yarn, sc 5 in magic loop [5]

Rnd 2: sc in each st around [5]

Fasten off and leave a long yarn tail. With a yarn needle and yarn tail, sew the beak to the head in between the eyes.

WINGS (MAKE 2)

Rnd 1: with **dark brown** yarn, sc 6 in magic loop [6]

Rnd 2: 2 sc in each st around [12]

Rnd 3: (sc 5, 2 sc in next st) repeat 2 times [14]

Rnds 4–5: sc in each st around [14]

Rnd 6: (sc 5, sc2tog) repeat 2 times [12]

Rnd 7: (sc 4, sc2tog) repeat 2 times [10]

Rnd 8: (sc 3, sc2tog) repeat 2 times [8]

Rnd 9: (sc2tog) repeat 4 times [4]

Do not stuff with fiberfill. Fasten off and leave a long yarn tail. With a yarn needle weave the tail through FLO to close opening, weave in ends.

Attach wings to either side of the body.

GINGERBREAD MAN

GINGER ALL THE WAY!

Materials

- 2.75mm (C/2) crochet hook
- Paintbox Yarns Cotton DK yarn: one 50g (1¾oz) ball each of Soft Fudge (**brown**), Paper White (**white**), and Red Wine (**red**)
- 7mm safety eyes
- Scraps of **black**, **white**, **red**, and **green** yarn
- Fiberfill stuffing
- Yarn needle
- Stitch marker

Finished Size

12.5cm (5in) tall by 9.5cm (3¾in) wide

Gauge

6 sc sts and 7 rows = 2.5cm (1in)

BODY AND HEAD

Rnd 1: with **brown** yarn, sc 6 in magic loop [6]

Rnd 2: 2 sc in each st around [12]

Rnd 3: (sc 1, 2 sc in next st) repeat 6 times [18]

Rnds 4–6: sc in each st around [18]

Rnd 7: (change to **white** yarn, sc 1, change to **brown** yarn, sc 1) repeat 9 times [18]

Rnd 8: change to **white** yarn, sc in each st around [18]

Rnd 9: change to **brown** yarn, sc in each st around [18]

Rnds 10–12: sc in each st around [18]

Invisible fasten off (see Finishing: Invisible Fasten Off) and weave in ends. Stuff with fiberfill.

Repeat **Rnds 1–12** for the second leg, do not fasten off.

Continue working in second leg to join the two legs together (1).

Rnd 13: sc 15, do not crochet in the next 3 sts, skip first 3 sts of the first leg, sc 15 [30]

Begin the next rnd in the next leg (2).

Rnds 14–21: sc in each st around [30]

Rnd 22: (sc 8, sc2tog) repeat 3 times [27]

Rnd 23: (sc 7, sc2tog) repeat 3 times [24]

Rnds 24–25: sc in each st around [24]

Rnd 26: (sc2tog) repeat 12 times [12]

Rnd 27: 2 sc in each st around [24]

Rnd 28: (sc 3, 2 sc in next st) repeat 6 times [30]

Rnd 29: (sc 9, 2 sc in next st) repeat 3 times [33]

Rnds 30–35: sc in each st around [33]

Place 7mm safety eyes between **Rnds 32 and 33** with 5 sts in between. Continue stuffing with fiberfill.

Rnd 36: (sc 9, sc2tog) repeat 3 times [30]

Rnd 37: (sc 3, sc2tog) repeat 6 times [24]

Rnd 38: (sc 2, sc2tog) repeat 6 times [18]

Rnd 39: (sc 1, sc2tog) repeat 6 times [12]

Rnd 40: (sc2tog) repeat 6 times [6]

Fasten off and leave a long yarn tail. With a yarn needle, weave the tail through FLO to close the opening. Fasten off and weave in ends.

Stitch the mouth and cheeks using **black** and **white** yarn (see Making Up: Stitching Facial Details).

ARMS (MAKE 2)

Rnd 1: with **brown** yarn, sc 6 in magic loop [6]

Rnd 2: 2 sc in each st around [12]

Rnd 3: (sc 3, 2 sc in next st) repeat 3 times [15]

Rnd 4: sc in each st around [15]

Rnd 5: (change to **white** yarn, sc 1, change to **brown** yarn, sc 1) repeat 7 times, change to **white** yarn, sc 1 [15]

Rnd 6: sc in each st around [15]

Rnd 7: change to **brown** yarn, sc in each st around [15]

Rnds 8–9: sc in each st around [15]

Fasten off and leave a long yarn tail. With the yarn tail, sew the arms to the body between **Rnds 19 and 23**.

BOWTIE

With **red** yarn, ch 5

Rnd 1: tr in 5th ch from hook, 2 tr in same st, ch 4, sl st in same st, turn work 90 degrees counterclockwise, ch 4, sl st in same st, 3 tr in same st, ch 4, sl st in same st [10]

Fasten off and leave a long yarn tail. Wrap the yarn tail around center of the bowtie three times. Attach the bowtie to the center of the neck.

FROSTING

Rnd 1: with **white** yarn, sc 6 in magic loop [6]

Rnd 2: 2 sc in each st around [12]

Rnd 3: (sc 1, ch 3, hdc in 2nd ch from hook, hdc in next ch, sc in same st as ch 3, sc 1, ch 2, hdc in 2nd ch from hook, sc in same st as ch 2, sc 2, ch 4, hdc in 2nd ch from hook, hdc in next 2 ch, sc in same st as ch 4, sc 2) repeat 2 times [30]

Invisible fasten off and weave in all ends. With a yarn needle and **red** and **green** yarn, sew small stitches on the frosting for the sprinkles. Attach the frosting to the top of the head.

The gingerbread man is one of England's most popular Christmas decorations. Its creation is attributed to Queen Elizabeth I, who is thought to have served gingerbread figurines to visiting dignitaries.

CHRISTMAS CANDLE

YOU LIGHT UP MY LIFE...

Materials

- 3.5mm (E/4) and 2.75mm (C/2) crochet hooks
- Paintbox Yarns Cotton Aran yarn: one 50g (1¾oz) ball each of Red Wine (**red**), Light Champagne (**white**), Blood Orange (**orange**), and Daffodil Yellow (**yellow**)
- Paintbox Yarns Cotton DK yarn: one 50g (1¾oz) ball each of Grass Green (**green**) and Red Wine (**red**)
- 8mm safety eyes
- Scraps of **black** and **orange** yarn
- Fiberfill stuffing
- Yarn needle
- Tapestry needle
- Stitch marker

Finished Size

14cm (5½in) tall by 5cm (2in) wide (without holly)

Gauge

5 sc sts and 6 rows = 2.5cm (1in) using Aran yarn

CANDLE

Rnd 1: with **3.5mm** hook and **red Aran** yarn, sc 6 in magic loop [6]

Rnd 2: 2 sc in each st around [12]

Rnd 3: (sc 1, 2 sc in next st) repeat 6 times [18]

Rnd 4: (sc 2, 2 sc in next st) repeat 6 times [24]

Rnd 5: working in BLO, sc in each st around [24]

Rnds 6–23: sc in each st around [24]

Place 8mm safety eyes between **Rnds 11 and 12** with 3 sts in between. Begin to stuff with fiberfill.

Rnd 24: working in BLO, (sc 2, sc2tog) 6 times [18]

Rnd 25: working in BLO, (sc 1, sc2tog) 6 times [12]

Rnd 26: (sc2tog) 6 times [6]

Fasten off and leave a long yarn tail. With yarn needle, weave the tail through FLO to close the opening.

Add stitches for mouth and cheeks using **black** and **orange** yarn (see Making Up: Stitching Facial Details).

Begin shaping by inserting tapestry teedle and yarn tail from center bottom to center top, insert needle back down from center top to slightly off-center bottom. Insert needle from center bottom to center top. Pull to create an indentation in the bottom of the Candle (see Making Up: Shaping). Fasten off and weave in ends.

MELTING WAX

Rnd 1: with **3.5mm** hook and **white Aran** yarn, sc 6 in magic loop [6]

Rnd 2: 2 sc in each st around [12]

Rnd 3: (sc 1, 2 sc in next st) repeat 6 times [18]

Rnd 4: (sc 1, 2 sc in next st) repeat 9 times [27]

Rnd 5: working in BLO, sc in each st around [27]

Rnd 6: (sc 3, sc 1 + ch 3 + sc in 2nd ch from hook + sc next ch st + sc in same st as ch 3, sc 1, sc 1 + ch 5 + sc in 2nd ch from hook + sc next 3 ch sts + sc in same st as ch 5, sc 2, sc 1 + ch 4 + sc in 2nd ch from hook + sc next 2 ch sts + sc in same st as ch 4) repeat 3 times [63]

Fasten off and weave in ends.

FLAME

Rnd 1: with **3.5mm** hook and **orange Aran** yarn, sc 7 in magic loop [7]

Rnd 2: change to **yellow Aran** yarn, sc 1, 2 hdc in next st, 2 dc in next st, dc 1 + tr 1 + dc 1 in next st, 2 dc in next st, 2 hdc in next st, sc 1 [13]

Fasten off and use yarn tails to tie flame to the center top of the melting wax. Attach the wax to the top of the candle.

HOLLY LEAVES (MAKE 2)

With **2.75mm** hook and **green DK** yarn, ch 10

Rnd 1: sc in 2nd ch from hook, sc 1, hdc 1, dc 1, 2 dc in next st, dc 1, hdc 1, sc 1, 3 sc in last ch st, working on the other side of the foundation ch, sc 1, hdc 1, dc 1, 2 dc in next st, dc 1, hdc 1, sc 2, sl st in skipped ch from beginning of ch 10 [22]

Rnd 2: (sl st 1, sc 1 + ch 2 + sl st in 2nd ch from hook + sc in same st as ch 2, sl st 1) repeat 7 times [35]

Fasten off and weave in ends. Attach to the base of the candle.

BERRIES (MAKE 3)

Rnd 1: with **2.75mm** hook and **red DK** yarn, sc 5 in magic loop [5]

Rnd 2: 2 sc in each st around [10]

Rnd 3: sc in each st around [10]

Rnd 4: (sc2tog) 5 times [5]

Stuff with fiberfill. Fasten off and leave a long yarn tail. With yarn needle, weave the tail through FLO to close the opening. Weave in all ends. Attach berries to the base of the candle in between the holly leaves.

Flame chart

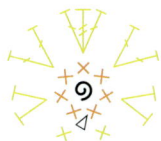

Leaf chart

MERRY CHRISTMAS PUDDING

TIME TO PUD UP THE DECORATIONS...

Materials

- 3.5mm (E/4) and 2.75mm (C/2) crochet hooks
- Paintbox Yarns Cotton Aran yarn: one 50g (1¾oz) ball each of Soft Fudge (**brown**), Champagne White (**white**), and Pillar Red (**red**)
- Paintbox Yarns Cotton DK yarn: one 50g (1¾oz) ball of Grass Green (**green**)
- 7mm safety eyes
- Scraps of **black** and **red** yarn
- Fiberfill stuffing
- Yarn needle
- Stitch marker

Finished Size

7.5cm (3in) tall by 7.5cm (3in) wide

Gauge

5 sc sts and 6 rows = 2.5cm (1in) using Aran yarn

PUDDING

Rnd 1: with **3.5mm** hook and **brown Aran** yarn, sc 6 in magic loop [6]

Rnd 2: 2 sc in each st around [12]

Rnd 3: (sc 1, 2 sc in next st) repeat 6 times [18]

Rnd 4: (sc 2, 2 sc in next st) repeat 6 times [24]

Rnd 5: (sc 3, 2 sc in next st) repeat 6 times [30]

Rnd 6: (sc 4, 2 sc in next st) repeat 6 times [36]

Rnd 7: (sc 5, 2 sc in next st) repeat 6 times [42]

Rnds 8–15: sc in each st around [42]

Place 7mm safety eyes between **Rnds 10 and 11** with 4 sts in between, begin to stuff with fiberfill.

Rnd 16: working in BLO, (sc 5, sc2tog) repeat 6 times [36]

Rnd 17: (sc 4, sc2tog) repeat 6 times [30]

Rnd 18: (sc 3, sc2tog) repeat 6 times [24]

Rnd 19: (sc 2, sc2tog) repeat 6 times [18]

Rnd 20: (sc 1, sc2tog) repeat 6 times [12]

Rnd 21: (sc2tog) repeat 6 times [6]

Finish stuffing with fiberfill. Fasten off and leave a long yarn tail. With a yarn needle and the tail, weave through FLO to close opening, weave in ends.

Stitch the mouth and cheeks using **black** and **red** yarn (see Making Up: Stitching Facial Details).

ICING

Rnd 1: with **3.5mm** hook and **white Aran** yarn, sc 6 in magic loop [6]

Rnd 2: 2 sc in each st around [12]

Rnd 3: (sc 1, 2 sc in next st) repeat 6 times [18]

Rnd 4: (sc 2, 2 sc in next st) repeat 6 times [24]

Rnd 5: (sc 3, 2 sc in next st) repeat 6 times [30]

Rnd 6: (sc 4, 2 sc in next st) repeat 6 times [36]

Rnd 7: (sc 5, 2 sc in next st) repeat 6 times [42]

Rnd 8: (sc 1, hdc 1, dc 1, 2 tr in next st, dc 1, hdc 2, dc 1, tr 1, 2 tr in next st, tr 1, dc 1, hdc 1, sc 1) repeat 3 times [48]

Fasten off and leave a long tail for sewing the icing onto the pudding.

HOLLY LEAVES (MAKE 3)

Rnd 1: with **2.75mm** hook and **green DK** yarn, ch 10, sc in 2nd ch from hook, sc 1, hdc 1, dc 1, 2 dc in next st, dc 1, hdc 1, sc 1, 3 sc in last ch, working on the other side of the foundation ch, sc 1, hdc 1, dc 1, 2 dc in next st, dc 1, hdc 1, sc 2, sl st in skipped ch from beginning of ch 10 [22]

Rnd 2: (sl st 1, sc 1 + ch 2 + sl st in 2nd ch from hook + sc in same st as ch 2, sl st 1) repeat 7 times, sl st 1, ch 6, sl st in 2nd ch from hook and remaining 4 ch sts, sl st 1 [42]

Leaf chart

Fasten off and weave in ends. Make a total of three holly leaves and attach them to the top of the icing.

BERRIES (MAKE 3)

Rnd 1: with **3.5mm** hook and **red Aran** yarn, sc 5 in magic loop [5]

Rnd 2: 2 sc in each st around [10]

Rnd 3: sc in each st around [10]

Rnd 4: (sc2tog) repeat 5 times [5]

Stuff with fiberfill. Fasten off and leave a long yarn tail. With a yarn needle weave the tail through FLO to close opening, weave in ends.

Make a total of three berries and attach them to the top of the icing.

EGGNOG

I'M SO EGG-CITED FOR THE HOLIDAYS!

Materials

- 3.5mm (E/4) and 2.75mm (C/2) crochet hooks
- Paintbox Yarns Cotton Aran yarn: one 50g (1¾oz) ball each of Daffodil Yellow (**yellow**) and Paper White (**white**)
- Paintbox Yarns Cotton DK yarn: one 50g (1¾oz) ball each of Coffee Bean (**brown**) and Paper White (**white**)
- 8mm and 5mm safety eyes
- Scraps of **black** and **red** yarn
- Fiberfill stuffing
- Yarn needle
- Tapestry needle
- Stitch marker

Finished Size

10.5cm (4¼in) tall by 10.5cm (4¼in) wide

Gauge

5 sc sts and 6 rows = 2.5cm (1in) using Aran yarn

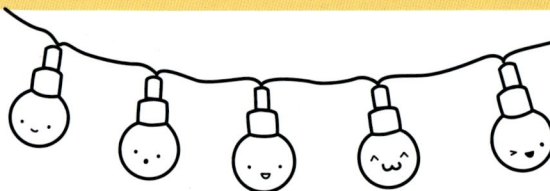

CUP

Rnd 1: with **3.5mm** hook and **yellow Aran** yarn, sc 6 in magic loop [6]

Rnd 2: 2 sc in each st around [12]

Rnd 3: (sc 1, 2 sc in next st) repeat 6 times [18]

Rnd 4: (sc 2, 2 sc in next st) repeat 6 times [24]

Rnd 5: (sc 3, 2 sc in next st) repeat 6 times [30]

Rnd 6: (sc 4, 2 sc in next st) repeat 6 times [36]

Rnds 7–16: sc in each st around [36]

Do not fasten off. Place 8mm safety eyes between **Rnds 13 and 14** with 4 sts in between. Begin to stuff with fiberfill. Make the eggnog before moving on to **Rnd 17**.

Rnd 17: Place the eggnog in the cup and line up the stitches from **Rnd 16** of the cup with **Rnd 6** of the eggnog. With **white Aran** yarn, sc in each st around working in both loops of both pieces to join them together [36]

Rnds 18–20: sc in each st around [36]

Rnd 21: sl st in each st around [36]

Invisible fasten off (see Finishing: Invisible Fasten Off) and weave in ends. Add stitches for the mouth and cheeks using **black** and **red** yarn (see Making Up: Stitching Facial Details). Thread a yarn needle with the **yellow Aran** yarn and begin shaping by inserting the needle from center bottom to center top, insert needle back down from center top to slightly off-center bottom. Insert needle from center bottom to center top. Pull to create an indentation in the bottom of the cup (see Making Up: Shaping). Fasten off and weave in ends.

HANDLE

Rnd 1: with **3.5mm** hook and **white Aran** yarn, sc 5 in magic loop [5]

Rnds 2–17: sc in each st around [5]

Do not stuff with fiberfill. Fasten off and leave a long yarn tail. With a yarn needle, weave the tail through FLO to close the opening. Fasten off and weave in ends. Attach to the side of the cup.

EGGNOG

Rnd 1: with **3.5mm** hook and **yellow Aran** yarn, sc 6 in magic loop [6]

Rnd 2: 2 sc in each st around [12]

Rnd 3: (sc 1, 2 sc in next st) repeat 6 times [18]

Rnd 4: (sc 2, 2 sc in next st) repeat 6 times [24]

Rnd 5: (sc 3, 2 sc in next st) repeat 6 times [30]

Rnd 6: (sc 4, 2 sc in next st) repeat 6 times [36]

Invisible fasten off and weave in ends.

WHIPPED CREAM

Rnd 1: with **2.75mm** hook and **white DK** yarn, sc 8 in magic loop [8]

Rnds 2–3: sc in each st around [8]

Rnd 4: 2 sc in each st around [16]

Rnd 5: sc in each st around [16]

Rnd 6: (sc 1, 2 sc in next st) repeat 8 times [24]

Rnd 7: sc in each st around [24]

Rnd 8: (sc 1, sc2tog) repeat 8 times [16]

Rnd 9: 2 sc in each st around [32]

Rnds 10–11: sc in each st around [32]

Place 5mm safety eyes between **Rnds 6 and 7** with 4 sts in between. Begin to stuff with fiberfill.

Rnd 12: working in BLO, (sc 2, sc2tog) repeat 8 times [24]

Rnd 13: (sc 1, sc2tog) repeat 8 times [16]

Rnd 14: (sc2tog) repeat 8 times [8]

Fasten off and leave a long yarn tail. With a yarn needle, weave the tail through FLO to close the opening. Fasten off and weave in ends. Stitch on mouth and cheeks using **black** and **red** yarn. Attach the whipped cream to the top of the cup.

CINNAMON STICKS (MAKE 2)

Rnd 1: with **2.75mm** hook and **brown DK** yarn, sc 7 in magic loop [7]

Rnd 2: working in BLO, sc in each st around [7]

Rnds 3–8: sc in each st around [7]

Stuff lightly with fiberfill. Fasten off and leave a long yarn tail. With yarn needle, weave tail through FLO to close the opening. Fasten off and weave in ends. Attach to the top of the cup.

Did you know eggnog was once called Posset? Most culinary historians agree that eggnog originated from the early medieval British drink called Posset, which was made with hot milk that was curdled with wine or ale and flavored with spices.

CHRISTMAS MOUSE

Materials

- 2.75mm (C/2) crochet hook
- Paintbox Yarns Cotton DK yarn: one 50g (1¾oz) ball each of Misty Grey (**gray**), Paper White (**white**), and Red Wine (**red**)
- 5mm safety eyes
- Fiberfill stuffing
- Yarn needle
- Tapestry needle
- Stitch marker

Finished Size

7.5cm (3in) long (including tail) by 3cm (1¼in) wide

Gauge

6 sc sts and 7 rows = 2.5cm (1in)

MERRY CHRISTMOUSE!

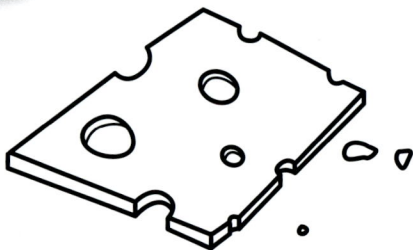

HEAD AND BODY

Rnd 1: with **gray** yarn, sc 6 in magic loop [6]

Rnd 2: (sc 2, 2 sc in next st) repeat 2 times [8]

Rnd 3: (sc 3, 2 sc in next st) repeat 2 times [10]

Rnd 4: (sc 4, 2 sc in next st) repeat 2 times [12]

Rnd 5: (sc 3, 2 sc in next st) repeat 3 times [15]

Rnd 6: (sc 4, 2 sc in next st) repeat 3 times [18]

Place 5mm safety eyes between **Rnds 3 and 4** with 2 sts in between. Begin to stuff with fiberfill.

Rnds 7–8: sc in each st around [18]

Rnd 9: (sc 4, sc2tog) repeat 3 times [15]

Rnd 10: sc in each st around [15]

Rnd 11: (sc 3, sc2tog) repeat 3 times [12]

Rnd 12: ch 11, sl st in 2nd ch from hook, sl st in next 9 ch sts, sl st in same st as ch 11 [10]

Fasten off and leave a long yarn tail. With a yarn needle, weave the tail through FLO to close the opening. Fasten off and weave in ends.

EARS (MAKE 2)

Rnd 1: with **gray** yarn, sc 6 in magic loop [6]

Rnd 2: 2 sc in each st around [12]

Sl st in next st. Fasten off and leave a long yarn tail for sewing. Sew ears to **Rnd 6** of the head and body.

SANTA HAT

Rnd 1: with **red** yarn, sc 4 in magic loop [4]

Rnd 2: (sc 1, 2 sc in next st) repeat 2 times [6]

Rnds 3–4: sc in each st around [6]

Rnd 5: (sc 1, 2 sc in next st) repeat 3 times [9]

Rnd 6: sc in each st around [9]

Rnd 7: (sc 2, 2 sc in next st) repeat 3 times [12]

Rnd 8: change to **white** yarn, (sc 3, 2 sc in next st) repeat 3 times [15]

Rnd 9: working in FLO, sc in each st around [15]

Fasten off and weave in ends.

POM-POM

Rnd 1: with **white** yarn, sc 5 in magic loop [5]

Rnd 2: sc in each st around [5]

Fasten off and leave a long yarn tail. With a yarn needle, weave the tail through FLO to close the opening. Fasten off and weave in ends. Attach pom-pom to **Rnd 1** of Santa hat. Attach Santa hat to the top of the mouse.

gift tags

> YOU'RE SO "SPEC-TAG-ULAR!"

TAGS (MAKE 3)

With **3.5mm** hook and and **dark green**, **red**, or **lime green Aran** yarn, ch 11

Row 1: sc in 2nd ch from hook, sc 9, turn [10]

Rows 2–11: ch 1, sc 10, turn [10]

Row 12: ch 1, sc2tog, sc 6, sc2tog, turn [8]

Row 13: ch 1, sc2tog, sc 4, sc2tog, turn [6]

Row 14: ch 1, sc2tog, ch 2, skip next 2 sts, sc2tog [4]

Rnd 15: sc around entire tag making 2 sc sts in each corner and 2 sc sts in the ch-2 space.

Invisible fasten off (see Finishing: Invisible Fasten Off) and weave in ends.

Repeat **Rows 1–14** and **Rnd 15** for a second tag. Each tag design requires two tag pieces to be stitched together.

Attach the reindeer, snowflake, or tree (see opposite) to the first tag and place the second tag behind the first before moving on to **Rnd 16**.

Rnd 16: join the same yarn color as the tag anywhere in **Rnd 15** and sl st around entire tag, inserting hook through both tags to join them together

Fasten off and weave in ends. Attach the ribbon to the top of the tag in the ch-2 space.

REINDEER APPLIQUÉ

With **2.75mm** hook and **brown DK** yarn, ch 7

Rnd 1: sc in 2nd ch from hook, sc 2, hdc 1, dc 1, 7 dc in last ch st, working on the other side of the foundation chain, dc 1, hdc 1, sc 3 [17]

Rnd 2: 2 sc in next st, sc 4, 2 sc in next st, sc 1, 2 sc in next 3 sts, sc 1, 2 sc in next st, sc 4, 2 sc in next st [24]

Rnd 3: sl st 2, ch 4, hdc in 3rd ch from hook, sc in next ch st, sl st 21, ch 4, hdc in 3rd ch from hook, sc 1 in next ch st, sl st 1 [28]

Place 5mm safety eyes between **Rnds 1 and 2** with 1 st in between.

Invisible fasten off and weave in ends. Stitch the mouth using **black** yarn (see Making Up: Stitching Facial Details). After attaching the nose and horns, attach to the **dark green** tag.

REINDEER NOSE

Rnd 1: with **2.75mm** hook and **red DK** yarn, sc 6 in magic loop [6]

Invisible fasten off and weave in ends. Attach to the reindeer.

RIGHT HORN

With **2.75mm** hook and **dark brown DK** yarn, ch 6

Row 1: sl st in 2nd ch from hook, sl st 2, ch 3, sl st in 2nd ch from hook, sl st in next ch st, working in the remaining 2 ch sts from ch 6, sl st 2 [7]

Fasten off and weave in ends.

LEFT HORN

With **2.75mm** hook and **dark brown DK** yarn, ch 5

Row 1: sl st in 2nd ch from hook, sl st 1, ch 4, sl st in 2nd ch from hook, sl st 2, working in remaining 2 ch sts from ch 6, sl st 2 [7]

Fasten off and weave in ends. Attach both horns to the top of the reindeer.

SNOWFLAKE APPLIQUÉ

Rnd 1: with **2.75mm** hook and **white DK** yarn, sc 6 in magic loop [6]

Rnd 2: 2 sc in each st around [12]

Rnd 3: (sl st in next st, ch 5, sl st in 4th ch from hook + ch 3 + sl st 1 + ch 3 + sl st 1, sl st in next st) repeat 6 times [30]

Invisible fasten off and weave in ends. Place 5mm safety eyes between **Rnds 1 and 2** with 2 sts in between. Stitch the mouth using **black** yarn (see Making Up: Stitching Facial Details).

Attach the snowflake to the **red** tag.

TREE APPLIQUÉ

With **2.75mm** hook and **green DK** yarn, ch 2

Row 1: sc in 2nd ch from hook, turn [1]

Row 2: ch 1, 2 sc in st, turn [2]

Row 3: ch 1, 2 sc in next st, sc 1, turn [3]

Row 4: ch 1, 2 sc in next st, sc 2, turn [4]

Row 5: ch 1, 2 sc in next st, sc 3, turn [5]

Row 6: ch 1, 2 sc in next st, sc 4, turn [6]

Row 7: ch 1, 2 sc in next st, sc 5, turn [7]

Row 8: ch 1, 2 sc in next st, sc 6, turn [8]

Row 9: ch 1, sc in each st across, turn [8]

Row 10: ch 1, 2 sc in next st, sc 7, turn [9]

Row 11: ch 1, 2 sc in next st, sc 8, turn [10]

Row 12: ch 1, sc in each st across, turn [10]

Place 5mm safety eyes between **Rows 8 and 9** with 2 sts in between. Stitch the mouth using **black** yarn.

Invisible fasten off and weave in ends.

TREE TRUNK

With **2.75mm** hook and **brown DK** yarn, ch 4

Row 1: sc in 2nd ch from hook, sc 2, turn [3]

Rows 2–3: ch 1, sc in each st across [3]

Invisible fasten off and weave in ends. Attach to the bottom of the tree. After attaching the trunk to the tree, attach the tree to the **lime green** tag.

BRUSSELS SPROUT

EVERY DAY I'M BRUSSELIN...

Materials

- 3.5mm (E/4) crochet hook
- Paintbox Yarns Cotton Aran yarn: one 50g (1¾oz) ball of Grass Green (**green**)
- 7mm safety eyes
- Scraps of **pink** and **black** yarn
- Fiberfill stuffing
- T-pins
- Yarn needle
- Stitch marker

Finished Size

6.5cm (2½in) tall by 6.5cm (2½in) wide

Gauge

5 sc sts and 6 rows = 2.5cm (1in)

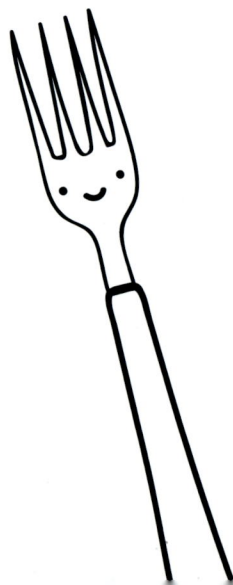

BRUSSELS SPROUT

Rnd 1: with **green** yarn, sc 6 in magic loop [6]

Rnd 2: 2 sc in each st around [12]

Rnd 3: (sc 1, 2 sc in next st) 6 times [18]

Rnd 4: (sc 2, 2 sc in next st) 6 times [24]

Rnd 5: (sc 3, 2 sc in next st) 6 times [30]

Rnds 6–10: sc in each st around [30]

Place 7mm safety eyes between **Rnds 4 and 5** with 3 sts in between. Begin to stuff with fiberfill.

Rnd 11: (sc 3, sc2tog) 6 times [24]

Rnd 12: (sc 2, sc2tog) 6 times [18]

Rnd 13: (sc 1, sc2tog) 6 times [12]

Rnd 14: (sc2tog) 6 times [6]

Finish stuffing. Fasten off and leave a long yarn tail. With a yarn needle, weave the tail through FLO to close the opening. Weave in all ends.

Add stitches for the mouth and cheeks using **black** and **pink** yarn (see Making Up: Stitching Facial Details).

LEAVES (MAKE 3)

Rnd 1: with **green** yarn, sc 6 in magic loop [6]

Rnd 2: 2 sc in each st around [12]

Rnd 3: (sc 1, 2 sc in next st) 6 times [18]

Rnd 4: (sc 2, 2 sc in next st) 6 times [24]

Rnd 5: (sc 3, 2 sc in next st) 6 times [30]

Rnd 6: sc in each st around [30]

Invisible fasten off (see Finishing: Invisible Fasten Off) and weave in all ends.

Pin the leaves into place and then attach to the brussels sprout, leaving the tops of the leaves unattached so they can be folded down (1–3).

Make a whole bowl full of sprouts for a cute centerpiece at Christmas.

TURKEY LEG

YOU HOLD THE TUR-KEY TO MY HEART

Materials

- 3.5mm (E/4) crochet hook
- Hobby Lobby I Love This Cotton (Aran/Medium) yarn: one 100g (3½oz) ball each of Ivory (**cream**) and Antique Gold (**brown**)
- 8mm safety eyes
- Scraps of **black** and **tan** yarn
- Fiberfill stuffing
- Yarn needle
- Stitch marker

Finished Size

15cm (6in) tall by 7.5cm (3in) wide

Gauge

5 sc sts and 6 rows = 2.5cm (1in)

TURKEY LEG

Rnd 1: with **cream** yarn, sc 6 in magic loop [6]

Rnd 2: 2 sc in each st around [12]

Rnds 3–4: sc in each st around [12]

Invisible fasten off (see Finishing: Invisible Fasten Off) and weave in ends.

Repeat **Rnds 1–4** for a second bone piece. Do not fasten off the second piece (1).

Connect the two bone pieces by placing piece 1 in front of piece 2. Insert hook in both pieces (2).

Rnd 5: working in both pieces, sc 2, working in the last st and the next st of piece 2, sc2tog, continue working around piece 2, sc 8, sc2tog, working in the first joining st of piece 1 and the next st of piece 1, sc2tog, continue working around piece 1, sc 8, sc2tog [20] (3 and 4).

Rnd 6: (sc 3, sc2tog) repeat 4 times [16]

Rnd 7: (sc 2, sc2tog) repeat 4 times [12]

Rnds 8–11: sc in each st around [12]

Begin to stuff with fiberfill.

Rnd 12: change to **brown** yarn, sc in each st around [12]

Rnd 13: working in BLO, sc in each st around [12]

Rnd 14: (sc 2, 2 sc in next st) repeat 4 times [16]

Rnd 15: sc in each st around [16]

Rnd 16: (sc 3, 2 sc in next st) repeat 4 times [20]

Rnd 17: sc in each st around [20]

Rnd 18: (sc 4, 2 sc in next st) repeat 4 times [24]

Rnd 19: sc in each st around [24]

Rnd 20: (sc 5, 2 sc in next st) repeat 4 times [28]

Rnd 21: sc in each st around [28]

Rnd 22: (sc 6, 2 sc in next st) repeat 4 times [32]

Rnd 23: sc in each st around [32]

Rnd 24: (sc 7, 2 sc in next st) repeat 4 times [36]

Rnd 25: sc in each st around [36]

Rnd 26: (sc 8, 2 sc in next st) repeat 4 times [40]

Rnds 27–29: sc in each st around [40]

Place 8mm safety eyes between **Rnds 26 and 27** with 5 sts in between. Begin to stuff with fiberfill.

Rnd 30: (sc 3, sc2tog, sc 3) repeat 5 times [35]

Rnd 31: (sc 5, sc2tog) repeat 5 times [30]

Rnd 32: (sc 2, sc2tog, sc 2) repeat 5 times [25]

Rnd 33: (sc 3, sc2tog) repeat 5 times [20]

Rnd 34: (sc 1, sc2tog, sc 1) repeat 5 times [15]

Rnd 35: (sc 1, sc2tog) repeat 5 times [10]

Rnd 36: (sc2tog) repeat 5 times [5]

Finish stuffing. Fasten off and leave a long yarn tail. With a yarn needle, weave the tail through FLO to close opening, weave in ends.

Rnd 37: working in FLO from **Rnd 13**, join **brown** yarn, (3 dc in next st, sl st 1) repeat 6 times

Stitch the mouth and cheeks using **black** and **tan** yarn (see Making Up: Stitching Facial Details).

TEDDY BEAR

UN-BEARABLY CUTE!

Materials

- 2.75mm (C/2) crochet hook
- Paintbox Yarns Cotton DK yarn: one 50g (1¾oz) ball each of Soft Fudge (**brown**), Champagne White (**white**), Spearmint Green (**green**), and Red Wine (**red**)
- Bernat Pipsqueak Chunky (Bulky) yarn (100% polyester): one 100g (3½oz) ball of Whitey White (**white novelty**)
- 6mm safety eyes
- Scrap of **black** yarn
- Fiberfill stuffing
- Yarn needle
- Stitch marker

Finished Size

12.5cm (5in) tall by 9.5cm (3¾in) wide

Gauge

6 sc sts and 7 rows = 2.5cm (1in)

BODY AND HEAD

Rnd 1: with **brown** yarn, sc 6 in magic loop [6]

Rnd 2: 2 sc in each st around [12]

Rnd 3: (sc 1, 2 sc in next st) repeat 6 times [18]

Rnds 4–5: sc in each st around [18]

Rnd 6: (sc 1, sc2tog) repeat 6 times [12]

Rnds 7–11: sc in each st around [12]

Invisible fasten off (see Finishing: Invisible Fasten Off) and weave in ends. Stuff first leg with fiberfill.

Repeat **Rnds 1–11** for a second leg, do not fasten off.

Continue working in second leg to join the two legs together.

Begin the next rnd in the next leg after making ch 3. (1 and 2)

Rnd 12: ch 3, sc 12, sc 3 along the chain (3), sc 12 around next leg (4), 2 sc in next ch st, sc 1, 2 sc in next ch st, along the back loops of the chain sts [32]

Rnd 13: (sc 7, 2 sc in next st) repeat 4 times [36]

Rnds 14–20: sc in each st around [36]

Rnd 21: (sc 4, sc2tog) repeat 6 times [30]

Rnd 20: sc in each st around [30]

Rnd 23: (sc 3, sc2tog) repeat 6 times [24]

Rnd 24: (sc 2, sc2tog) repeat 6 times [18]

Rnd 25: (sc 1, sc2tog) repeat 6 times [12]

Rnd 26: sc in each st around [12]

Rnd 27: 2 sc in each st around [24]

Rnd 28: (sc 1, 2 sc in next st) repeat 12 times [36]

Rnds 29–37: sc in each st around [36]

Place 6mm safety eyes between **Rnds 32 and 33** with 6 sts in between. Continue stuffing with fiberfill.

Rnd 38: (sc 4, sc2tog) repeat 6 times [30]

Rnd 39: (sc 3, sc2tog) repeat 6 times [24]

Rnd 40: (sc 2, sc2tog) repeat 6 times [18]

Rnd 41: (sc 1, sc2tog) repeat 6 times [12]

Rnd 42: (sc2tog) repeat 6 times [6]

Fasten off and leave a long yarn tail. With a yarn needle, weave the tail through FLO to close the opening. Fasten off and weave in ends.

MUZZLE

Rnd 1: with **white** yarn, sc 6 in magic loop [6]

Rnd 2: (sc 1, 2 sc in next st) repeat 3 times [9]

Rnd 3: sc in each st around [9]

Invisible fasten off and leave a long yarn tail. Stitch the nose and mouth using **black** yarn. With a yarn needle and yarn tail sew the muzzle onto the head between **Rnds 29 and 32**. Stuff with fiberfill.

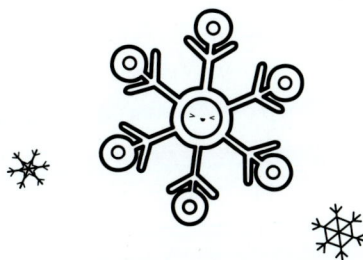

EARS (MAKE 2)

Row 1: with **brown** yarn, sc 6 in magic loop, turn [6]

Row 2: ch 1, (sc 1, 2 sc in next st) repeat 3 times, turn [9]

Row 3: ch 1, sc 9 [9]

Fasten off and leave a long yarn tail. Repeat **Rows 1–3** for a second ear.

With a yarn needle and yarn tail, sew the ears to each side of the head between **Rnds 34 and 39**. Weave in ends.

ARMS (MAKE 2)

Rnd 1: with **brown** yarn, sc 6 in magic loop, turn [6]

Rnd 2: 2 sc in each st around [12]

Rnds 3–5: sc in each st around [12]

Rnd 6: (sc2tog) repeat 3 times, sc 6 [9]

Rnds 7–12: sc in each st around [9]

Stuff lightly with fiberfill.

Fasten off and leave a long yarn tail. Sew the opening of the arm closed. Repeat **Rnds 1–12** for the second arm.

With a yarn needle and yarn tail sew the arms to each side of the body between **Rnds 23 and 24**. Weave in ends.

SANTA HAT

Rnd 1: with **red** yarn, sc 6 in magic loop, turn [6]

Rnd 2: (sc 1, 2 sc in next st) repeat 3 times [9]

Rnds 3–4: sc in each st around [9]

Rnd 5: (sc 2, 2 sc in next st) repeat 3 times [12]

Rnds 6–7: sc in each st around [12]

Rnd 8: (sc 3, 2 sc in next st) repeat 3 times [15]

Rnds 9–10: sc in each st around [15]

Rnd 11: (sc 4, 2 sc in next st) repeat 3 times [18]

Rnds 12–13: sc in each st around [18]

Rnd 14: (sc 2, 2 sc in next st) repeat 6 times [24]

Rnds 15–16: sc in each st around [24]

Rnd 17: (sc 3, 2 sc in next st) repeat 3 times [30]

Rnds 18–19: sc in each st around [30]

Rnd 20: (sc 4, 2 sc in next st) repeat 3 times [36]

Rnds 21–22: sc in each st around [36]

Rnd 23: change to **white novelty** yarn, working in FLO, sc in each st around [36]

Rnds 24–26: sc in each st around [36]

Invisible fasten off and weave in ends.

Fold white brim up.

POM-POM

Rnd 1: with **white novelty** yarn, sc 6 in magic loop [6]

Rnd 2: 2 sc in each st around [12]

Rnd 3: (sc2tog) repeat 6 times [6]

Fasten off and leave a long yarn tail. With a yarn needle, weave the tail through FLO to close the opening. Fasten off and weave in ends. Attach the pom-pom to **Rnd 1** of the Santa hat and bend the top of the hat down and secure at **Rnd 11**.

SCARF

With **red** yarn, ch 4

Row 1: sc in 2nd ch from hook, sc 2, turn [3]

Rows 2–3: ch 1, sc in each st across, turn [3]

Row 4: change to **green** yarn, ch 1, sc in each st across, turn [3]

Row 5: change to **red** yarn, ch 1, sc in each st across, turn [3]

Rows 6–7: ch 1, sc in each st across, turn [3]

Row 8: change to **green** yarn, ch 1, sc in each st across, turn [3]

Rows 9–56: repeat **Rows 5–8**

Row 57: change to **red** yarn, ch 1, sc in each st across, turn [3]

Rows 58–59: ch 1, sc in each st across, turn [3]

Fasten off and weave in ends.

CHRISTMAS CACTUS

WE WISH YOU A MERRY CACTUS...

Materials

- 3.5mm (E/4) and 2.75mm (C/2) crochet hooks
- Paintbox Yarns Cotton Aran yarn: one 50g (1¾oz) ball each of Pillar Red (**red**) and Soft Fudge (**brown**)
- Paintbox Yarns Cotton DK yarn: one 50g (1¾oz) ball each of Spearmint Green (**green**) and Pillar Red (**red**)
- Scraps of **black** and **pink** yarn
- 8mm safety eyes
- Fiberfill stuffing
- 26-gauge floral wire
- Yarn needle
- Stitch marker

Finished Size

19cm (7½in) tall by 18cm (7in) wide

Gauge

5 sc sts and 6 rows = 2.5cm (1in) using Aran yarn

6 sc sts and 7 rows = 2.5cm (1in) using DK yarn

POT

Rnd 1: with **3.5mm** hook and **red Aran** yarn, sc 6 in magic loop [6]

Rnd 2: 2 sc in each st around [12]

Rnd 3: (sc 1, 2 sc in next st) 6 times [18]

Rnd 4: (sc 2, 2 sc in next st) 6 times [24]

Rnd 5: (sc 3, 2 sc in next st) 6 times [30]

Rnd 6: (sc 4, 2 sc in next st) 6 times [36]

Rnd 7: (sc 5, 2 sc in next st) 6 times [42]

Rnd 8: working in BLO, sc in each st around [42]

Rnds 9–13: sc in each st around [42]

Rnd 14: (sc 6, 2 sc in next st) 6 times [48]

Rnds 15–17: sc in each st around [48]

Place 8mm safety eyes between **Rnds 13 and 14**, with 5 sts in between. Begin to stuff with fiberfill. Do not fasten off and cut yarn. Make the dirt before moving on to **Rnd 18**.

Rnd 18: place the dirt in the pot and line up the stitches from **Rnd 17** of the pot and **Rnd 8** of the dirt. With the yarn used to make the pot, sc in each st around, working in both loops of both pieces to join them together (see Making Up: Crocheting Two Pieces Together) [48]

Rnd 19: ch 1, sc in each st around, join with sl st in first st [48]

Rnd 20: sl st in each st around [48]

Invisible fasten off (see Finishing: Invisible Fasten Off) and weave in ends. Add stitches for the mouth and cheeks using **black** and **pink** yarn (see Making Up: Stitching Facial Details).

Begin shaping by inserting needle from center bottom to center top, then take needle back down from center top to slightly off-center bottom and back up to center top. Pull to create an indentation in the bottom of the pot (see Making Up: Shaping). Fasten off and weave in ends.

DIRT

Rnd 1: with **3.5mm** hook and **brown Aran** yarn, sc 6 in magic loop [6]

Rnd 2: 2 sc in each st around [12]

Rnd 3: (sc 1, 2 sc in next st) 6 times [18]

Rnd 4: (sc 2, 2 sc in next st) 6 times [24]

Rnd 5: (sc 3, 2 sc in next st) 6 times [30]

Rnd 6: (sc 4, 2 sc in next st) 6 times [36]

Rnd 7: (sc 5, 2 sc in next st) 6 times [42]

Rnd 8: (sc 6, 2 sc in next st) 6 times [48]

Invisible fasten off and weave in ends.

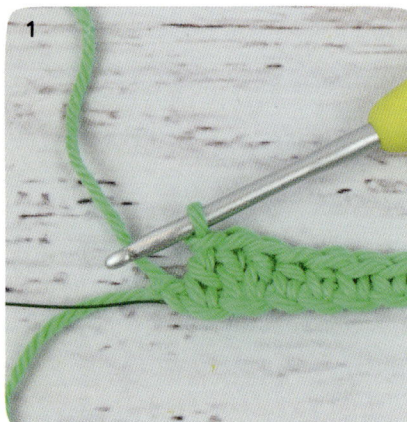

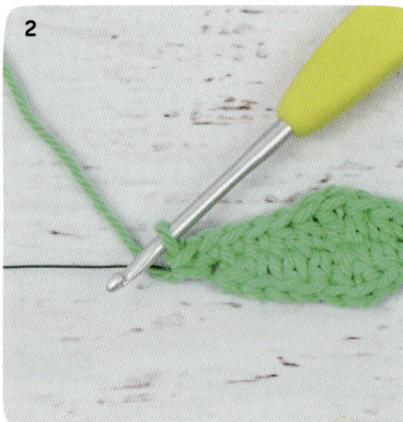

STEMS (MAKE 9)

Rnd 1: with **2.75mm** hook and **green DK** yarn, ch 16, cut a 15cm (6in) piece of floral wire, hold behind the foundation ch and crochet the following sts around the wire (see Making Up: Crocheting with Floral Wire): sc in 2nd ch from hook, sc 1, hdc 2, 2 dc in next st, hdc 1, sc 4, hdc 2, 2 dc in next st, hdc 1 (1), bend wire end behind sts, 3 sc in last st, working on the other side of the foundation ch, hdc 1, 2 dc in next st, hdc 2, sc 4, hdc 1, 2 dc in next st, hdc 2, sc 2, 2 sc in beginning skipped ch st (2) [37]

Rnd 2: sl st 4, ch-2 picot, sl st 2, ch-2 picot, sl st 7, ch-2 picot, sl st 2, ch-2 picot, sl st 5, ch-2 picot, sl st 2, ch-2 picot, sl st 3, sl st both sides of stem together by first inserting hook on the opposite side and then in the next st on the current side of the stem (3), sl st 3, ch-2 picot, sl st 2, ch-2 picot, sl st 6 [45]

Fasten off, leaving a long yarn tail for sewing the stem to the dirt.

BLOSSOMS (MAKE 9)

Rnd 1: with **2.75mm** hook and **red DK** yarn, sc 6 in magic loop [6]

Rnd 2: sc in each st around [6]

Rnd 3: (ch 3, hdc + dc + hdc in 3rd ch from hook, working in FLO, sc 2) 3 times [15]

Rnd 4: working in BLO from **Rnd 2**, sc in each st around [6]

Rnd 5: sc in each st around [6]

Rnd 6: (ch 3, hdc + dc + hdc in 3rd ch from hook, sc 2) 3 times [15]

Fasten off and weave in ends.

Attach a blossom to the end of each stem (4).

Push three stems into the center of the dirt and sew them to the dirt with yarn needle and yarn tail. Next, push six stems in a circle around the first three stems and sew in place. Bend the stems into a droopy position.

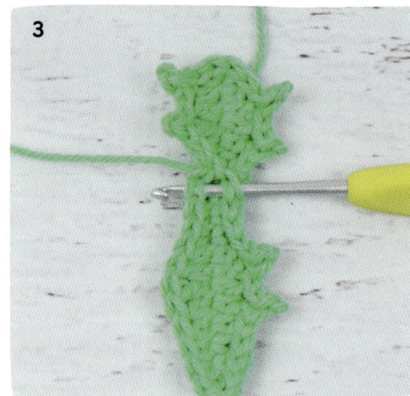

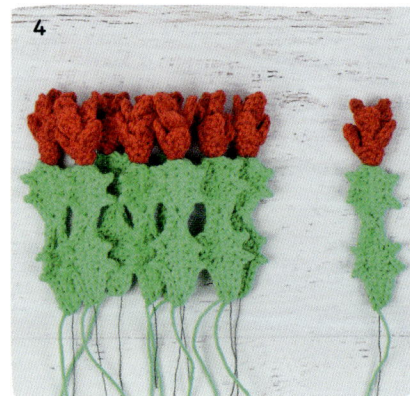

CANDY CANE

Materials

- 2.75mm (C/2) crochet hook
- Paintbox Yarns Cotton DK yarn: one 50g (1¾oz) ball each of Paper White (**white**) and Red Wine (**red**)
- 5mm safety eyes
- Scraps of **black** and **pink** yarn
- Fiberfill stuffing
- Yarn needle
- Stitch marker

Finished Size

12.5cm (5in) tall by 5.5cm (2¼in) wide

Gauge

6 sc sts and 7 rows = 2.5cm (1in)

WE WERE PEPPERMINT TO BE

CANDY CANE

Rnd 1: with **white** yarn, sc 6 in magic loop [6]

Rnd 2: 2 sc in each st around [12]

Rnd 3: sc in each st around [12]

Rnd 4: change to **red** yarn, sc in each st around [12]

Rnds 5–6: sc in each st around [12]

Begin stuffing with fiberfill.

Rnd 7: change to **white** yarn, sl st 6, sc 6 [12]

Rnds 8–9: sl st 6, sc 6 [12]

Rnd 10: change to **red** yarn, sc 1, sl st 6, sc 5 [12]

Rnds 11–12: sc 1, sl st 6, sc 5 [12]

Rnd 13: change to **white** yarn, sc 2, sl st 6, sc 4 [12]

Rnds 14–15: sc 2, sl st 6, sc 4 [12]

Rnd 16: change to **red** yarn, sc 3, sl st 6, sc 3 [12]

Rnds 17–18: sc 3, sl st 6, sc 3 [12]

Rnd 19: change to **white** yarn, sc 4, sl st 6, sc 2 [12]

Rnds 20–21: sc 4, sl st 6, sc 2 [12]

Rnd 22: change to **red** yarn, sc 5, sl st 6, sc 1 [12]

Rnds 23–24: sc 5, sl st 6, sc 1 [12]

Rnd 25: change to **white** yarn, sc 6, sl st 6 [12]

Rnds 26–27: sc 6, sl st 6 [12]

Rnd 28: change to **red** yarn, sc in each st around [12]

Rnds 29–30: sc in each st around [12]

Place 5mm safety eyes between **Rnds 28 and 29** with 2 sts in between. Continue stuffing with fiberfill.

Rnd 31: change to **white** yarn, sc in each st around [12]

Rnds 32–33: sc in each st around [12]

Rnd 34: change to **red** yarn, sc in each st around [12]

Rnds 35–36: sc in each st around [12]

Rnds 37–48: repeat **Rnds 31–36** twice

Rnd 49: change to **white** yarn, sc in each st around [12]

Rnd 50: sc in each st around [12]

Rnd 51: (sc2tog) repeat 6 times [6]

Fasten off and leave a long yarn tail. With a yarn needle, weave the tail through FLO to close the opening. Weave in ends.

Stitch the mouth and cheeks using **black** and **pink** yarn (see Making Up: Stitching Facial Details).

CHRISTMAS TREE

Materials

- 3.5mm (E/4) and 2.75mm (C/2) crochet hooks
- Paintbox Yarns Cotton Aran yarn: one 50g (1¾oz) ball each of Grass Green (**green**) and Coffee Bean (**brown**)
- Paintbox Yarns Cotton DK yarn: one 50g (1¾oz) ball of Buttercup Yellow (**yellow**)
- 7mm safety eyes
- Scraps of **light green** and **black** yarn
- Fiberfill stuffing
- Yarn needle
- Stitch marker

Finished Size

12.5cm (5in) tall by 6.5cm (2½in) wide

Gauge

5 sc sts and 6 rows = 2.5cm (1in) using Aran yarn

I'M PINE-ING FOR YOU

TREE

Rnd 1: with **3.5mm** hook and **brown Aran** yarn, sc 6 in magic loop [6]

Rnd 2: 2 sc in each st around [12]

Rnd 3: working in BLO, sc in each st around [12]

Rnds 4–7: sc in each st around [12]

Rnd 8: change to **green Aran** yarn, working in FLO, (sc 1, 2 sc in next st) 6 times [18]

Rnd 9: (sc 2, 2 sc in next st) 6 times [24]

Rnd 10: (sc 3, 2 sc in next st) 6 times [30]

Rnd 11: working in BLO, sc in each st around [30]

Rnds 12–13: sc in each st around [30]

Rnd 14: (sc 3, sc2tog) 6 times [24]

Rnds 15–16: sc in each st around [24]

Rnd 17: working in BLO, sc in each st around [24]

Place 7mm safety eyes between **Rnds 13 and 14** with 4 sts in between. Begin to stuff with fiberfill.

Rnd 18: (sc 2, sc2tog) 6 times [18]

Rnd 19: sc in each st around [18]

Rnd 20: working in BLO, sc in each st around [18]

Rnd 21: sc in each st around [18]

Rnd 22: (sc 1, sc2tog) 6 times [12]

Rnd 23: working in BLO, sc in each st around [12]

Rnds 24–25: sc in each st around [12]

Rnd 26: (sc2tog) 6 times [6]

Finish stuffing. Fasten off and leave a long yarn tail. With a yarn needle, weave the tail through FLO to close the opening. Weave in all ends.

Add stitches for the mouth and cheeks using **black** and **light green** yarn (see Making Up: Stitching Facial Details).

With the top of the tree pointing down, join **green Aran** yarn in any FLO from **Rnd 10**, working in FLO, (ch 2, sc 1) to end of rnd. Repeat the same in the front loops from **Rnds 16, 19, and 22**.

STAR

Rnd 1: with **2.75mm** hook and **yellow DK** yarn, sc 5 in magic loop [5]

Rnd 2: (ch 3, sl st in 2nd ch from hook, sc in next ch, sl st in next st from **Rnd 1**) 5 times

Invisible fasten off (see Finishing: Invisible Fasten Off) and weave in all ends. Attach the star to the top of the tree.

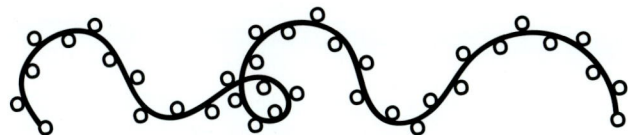

STRING LIGHTS

Materials

- 2.75mm (C/2) crochet hook
- Paintbox Yarns Cotton DK yarn: one 50g (1¾oz) ball each of Blood Orange (**orange**), Pillar Red (**red**), Raspberry Pink (**pink**), Sailor Blue (**blue**), Lime Green (**lime green**), Buttercup Yellow (**yellow**), and Grass Green (**green**)
- 5mm safety eyes
- Scraps of **orange**, **black**, **red**, **green**, **light blue**, and **pink** yarn
- Fiberfill stuffing
- Yarn needle
- Stitch marker

Finished Size

7.5cm (3in) tall by 4cm (1½in) wide

Gauge

5 sc sts and 6 rows = 2.5cm (1in)

LOVE AT FIRST LIGHT

LIGHTS (MAKE 1 IN EACH COLOR)

Rnd 1: with your choice of yarn color, sc 6 in magic loop [6]

Rnd 2: sc in each st around [6]

Rnd 3: (sc 1, 2 sc in next st) repeat 3 times [9]

Rnd 4: (sc 2, 2 sc in next st) repeat 3 times [12]

Rnd 5: (sc 3, 2 sc in next st) repeat 3 times [15]

Rnd 6: (sc 4, 2 sc in next st) repeat 3 times [18]

Rnd 7: (sc 5, 2 sc in next st) repeat 3 times [21]

Rnd 8: (sc 6, 2 sc in next st) repeat 3 times [24]

Rnd 9: (sc 3, 2 sc in next st) repeat 6 times [30]

Rnds 10–14: sc in each st around [30]

Place 5mm safety eyes between **Rnds 9 and 10** with 3 sts in between. Begin to stuff with fiberfill.

Rnd 15: (sc 3, sc2tog) repeat 6 times [24]

Rnd 16: (sc 2, sc2tog) repeat 6 times [18]

Rnd 17: sc in each st around [18]

Rnd 18: (sc 1, sc2tog) repeat 6 times [12]

Rnd 19: change to **green** yarn, sc in each st around [12]

Rnds 20–21: sc in each st around [12]

Rnd 22: working in BLO, (sc2tog) repeat 6 times [6]

Finish stuffing with fiberfill. Fasten off and leave a long yarn tail.

With a yarn needle weave the tail through FLO to close opening. Weave in all ends.

Stitch the mouth and cheeks using **black** and **red**, **orange**, **green**, **blue**, or **pink** yarn (see Making Up: Stitching Facial Details).

STRING

Make at least six different-colored lights, and, with **green** yarn, ch 10, sl st in 10th ch from hook, (ch 20, sl st in the top of a light) repeat until you have joined all your lights, ch 30, sl st in the 10th ch from hook. Fasten off and weave in ends. Tie a knot where both slip stitches were made at the beginning and end of the string of lights.

The history of Christmas lights can be traced back to medieval Germany, where the tradition of burning the Yule log during the winter brought light into homes.

CHRISTMAS TREE SUGAR COOKIE

Materials

- 3.5mm (E/4) crochet hook
- Paintbox Yarns Cotton Aran yarn: one 50g (1¾oz) ball each of Light Caramel (**tan**) and Spearmint Green (**green**)
- 8mm safety eyes
- Scrap of **black** yarn
- Fiberfill stuffing
- Yarn needle
- Stitch marker

Finished Size

11.5cm (4½in) tall by 7.5cm (3in) wide

Gauge

5 sc sts and 6 rows = 2.5cm (1in)

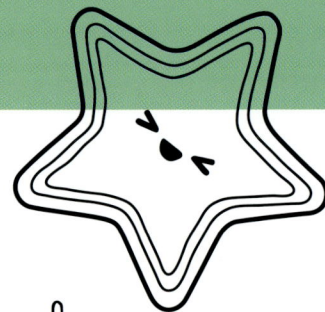

WE'RE A BATCH MADE IN HEAVEN!

FROSTING

With **green** yarn, ch 2

Row 1: sc in 2nd ch from hook, turn [1]

Row 2: ch 1, 2 sc in next st, turn [2]

Row 3: ch 1, sc 1, 2 sc in next st, turn [3]

Row 4: ch 1, sc 2, 2 sc in next st, turn [4]

Row 5: ch 1, sc 3, 2 sc in next st, turn [5]

Row 6: ch 1, sc 4, 2 sc in next st, turn [6]

Row 7: ch 1, sc 5, 2 sc in next st, turn [7]

Row 8: sl st 2 (sl st 1 + ch 1 + 2 sc) in next st, sc 1, 2 sc in next st, leave remaining sts unworked, turn [9]

Row 9: ch 1, 2 sc in next st, sc 3, 2 sc in next st, leave remaining sts unworked, turn [7]

Row 10: ch 1, sc 6, 2 sc in next st, turn [8]

Row 11: ch 1, sc 7, 2 sc in next st, turn [9]

Row 12: ch 1, sc 8, 2 sc in next st, turn [10]

Row 13: ch 1, sl st 2 (sl st + ch 1 + 2 sc) in next st, sc 4, 2 sc in next st, leave remaining sts unworked, turn [12]

Row 14: ch 1, 2 sc in next st, sc 6, 2 sc in next st, turn [10]

Row 15: ch 1, sc 9, 2 sc in next st, turn [11]

Row 16: ch 1, sc 10. 2 sc in next st, turn [12]

Row 17: ch 1, sc 11, 2 sc in next st, turn [13]

Row 18: sl st 5 (sl st + ch 1 + sc 1) in next st, sc 2, leave remaining sts unworked, turn [10]

Row 19: ch 1, sc 3 [3]

Fasten off and weave in ends.

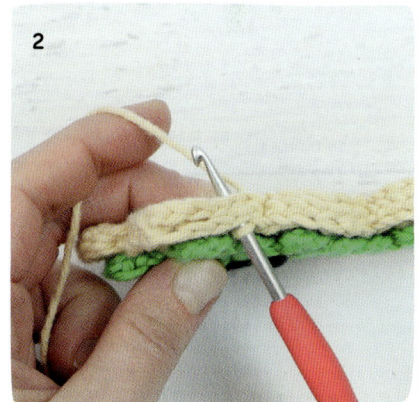

COOKIES (MAKE 2)

Rows 1–19: with **tan** yarn, repeat **Rows 1–19** of frosting

Rnd 20: sc in each st around making a ch 1 at each corner (1)

Fasten off.

Repeat **Rows 1–19** and **Rnd 20** for second cookie, do not fasten off yarn.

Place the frosting in the center of one of the cookies.

Place 8mm safety eyes between **Rows 13 and 14** of the frosting with 3 sts in between. Insert safety eyes in both layers of the frosting and cookie. Attach the frosting to the cookie.

Add stitches for the mouth using **black** yarn (see Making Up: Stitching Facial Details).

Rnd 21: place the second cookie layer behind the first. Do not stuff with fiberfill. With the yarn used to make the second cookie, sl st around the entire cookie inserting the hook through both cookie layers to join them together (2)

Fasten off and weave in ends.

MINI CHRISTMAS STOCKING

STOCKING UP ON OUR FAVORITE HOLIDAY TRADITIONS...

Materials

- 3.5mm (E/4) crochet hook
- Paintbox Yarns Cotton Aran yarn: one 50g (1¾oz) ball each of Pillar Red (**red**) and Paper White (**white**)
- 7mm safety eyes
- Scraps of **pink** and **black** yarn
- Fiberfill stuffing
- Yarn needle
- Stitch marker

Finished Size

14cm (5½in) tall by 7.5cm (3in) wide

Gauge

5 sc sts and 6 rows = 2.5cm (1in)

STOCKING

Rnd 1: with **white** yarn, sc 6 in magic loop [6]

Rnd 2: 2 sc in each st around [12]

Rnd 3: (sc 1, 2 sc in next st) repeat 6 times [18]

Rnds 4–6: sc in each st around [18]

Rnd 7: change to **red** yarn, sc in each st around [18]

Rnds 8–12: sc in each st around [18]

Do not fasten off **red** yarn.

The next 5 rows you will be working rows instead of rounds and will be making the heel of the stocking. **Row 13** is not a complete rnd.

Row 13: change to **white** yarn, sc 9, turn [9]

Rows 14–17: ch 1, sc 9, turn [9]

Fasten off **white** yarn and leave a long yarn tail. With a yarn needle, sew **Row 17** together to close the heel. (1)

Now start working in rounds again.

Rnd 18: change to **red** yarn, sc around **Rnd 12** and the side loops of the stitches from the heel [18] (2)

Rnds 19–25: sc in each st around [18]

Place 7mm safety eyes between **Rnds 23 and 24** with 3 sts in between. Begin to stuff lightly with fiberfill.

Rnd 26: change to **white** yarn, sc in each st around [18]

Rnds 27–28: sc in each st around [18]

Rnd 29: sl st in each st around. When directly above the heel, create a hanging loop: ch 14, sl st in 2nd ch from hook, sl st in remaining ch sts, insert hook in ch 14 and also next st of stocking, continuing sl st around [31] (3)

Fasten off and leave a long yarn tail. With a yarn needle and the tail, sew the top opening of the stocking closed (4). Fasten off and weave in ends.

Stitch the mouth and cheeks using **black** and **pink** yarn (see Making Up: Stitching Facial Details).

Optional: Create a functional mini Christmas stocking by not stuffing with fiberfill and not stitching the opening closed.

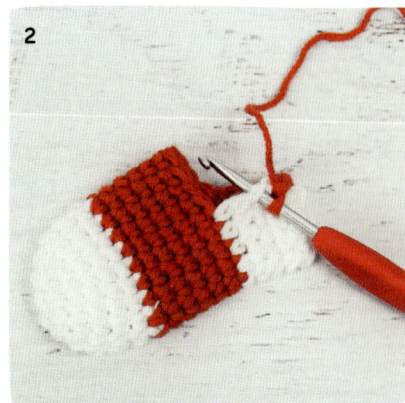

The Christmas stocking tradition is thought to have originated from the life of St Nicholas. One popular legend tells the story of a 4th-century widower with three daughters who couldn't afford dowries. St Nicholas secretly dropped three gold spheres down the chimney, which landed in the daughters' stockings. Because of that legend, on Christmas Eve, children in Scandinavia leave their shoes on the hearth, while children in the US and the UK leave their stockings on their bedpost or near the fireplace in hopes it will be filled with treats.

SANTA'S MILK AND COOKIES

FRIEND-CHIP GOALS...

Materials

- 3.5mm (E/4) crochet hook
- Paintbox Yarns Cotton Aran yarn: one 50g (1¾oz) ball each of Duck Egg Blue (**light blue**), Champagne White (**white**), Light Caramel (**tan**), Grass Green (**green**), and Pillar Red (**red**)
- 9mm and 7mm safety eyes
- Scraps of **brown**, **black**, and **pink** yarn
- Fiberfill stuffing
- Yarn needle
- Stitch marker

Finished Size

Milk: 11.5cm (4½in) tall by 10cm (4in) wide

Cookie: 7.5cm (3in) in diameter

Gauge

5 sc sts and 6 rows = 2.5cm (1in)

MILK

Rnd 1: with **white** yarn, sc 6 in magic loop [6]

Rnd 2: 2 sc in each st around [12]

Rnd 3: (sc 1, 2 sc in next st) repeat 6 times [18]

Rnd 4: (sc 2, 2 sc in next st) repeat 6 times [24]

Rnd 5: (sc 3, 2 sc in next st) repeat 6 times [30]

Rnd 6: (sc 4, 2 sc in next st) repeat 6 times [36]

Rnd 7: (sc 5, 2 sc in next st) repeat 6 times [42]

Rnd 8: (sc 6, 2 sc in next st) repeat 6 times [48]

Rnd 9: (sc 7, 2 sc in next st) repeat 6 times [54]

Invisible fasten off (see Finishing: Invisible Fasten Off) and weave in ends.

GLASS OF MILK

Rnd 1: with **light blue**, sc 6 in magic loop [6]

Rnd 2: 2 sc in each st around [12]

Rnd 3: (sc 1, 2 sc in next st) repeat 6 times [18]

Rnd 4: (sc 2, 2 sc in next st) repeat 6 times [24]

Rnd 5: (sc 3, 2 sc in next st) repeat 6 times [30]

Rnd 6: (sc 4, 2 sc in next st) repeat 6 times [36]

Rnd 7: (sc 5, 2 sc in next st) repeat 6 times [42]

Rnd 8: working in BLO, sc in each st around [42]

Rnd 9: change to **white** yarn, sc in each st around [42]

Rnds 10–15: sc in each st around [42]

Rnd 16: (sc 13, 2 sc in next st) repeat 3 times [45]

Rnds 17–20: sc in each st around [45]

Rnd 21: (sc 14, 2 sc in next st) repeat 3 times [48]

Rnds 22–24: sc in each st around [48]

Rnd 25: (sc 7, 2 sc in next st) repeat 6 times [54]

Place 9mm safety eyes between **Rnds 20 and 21** with 5 sts in between.

Begin to stuff with fiberfill. Do not fasten off and cut yarn.

Rnd 26: change to **light blue** yarn, place the milk in the cup and line up the stitches from **Rnd 25** of the cup and **Rnd 9** of the milk, sc in each st around working in both loops of both pieces to join them together, join with sl st in first st [54]

Rnd 27: (sc 16, sc2tog) repeat 3 times [51]

Rnds 28–31: sc in each st around [51]

Rnd 32: sl st in each st around [51]

Invisible fasten off and weave in ends.

Add stitches for the mouth and cheeks using **black** and **pink** yarn (see Making Up: Stitching Facial Details).

With **light blue** yarn, begin shaping by inserting a yarn needle from center bottom to center top, insert needle back down from center top to slightly off-center bottom. Insert needle from center bottom to center top. Pull to create an indentation in the bottom of the cup (see Making Up: Shaping). Fasten off and weave in ends.

HOLLY LEAVES (MAKE 2)

With **green** yarn, ch 10

Rnd 1: sc in 2nd ch from hook, sc 1, hdc 1, dc 1, 2 dc in next st, dc 1, hdc 1, sc 1, 3 sc in last ch st, working on the other side of the foundation ch, sc 1, hdc 1, dc 1, 2 dc in next st, dc 1, hdc 1, sc 2, sl st in skipped ch from beginning of ch 10 [22]

Rnd 2: (sl st 1, sc 1 + ch 2 + sl st in 2nd ch from hook + sc in same st as ch 2, sl st 1) repeat 7 times, sl st 1, ch 6, sl st in 2nd ch from hook and remaining 4 ch sts, sl st 1 [42]

Fasten off and weave in ends. Repeat **Rnds 1–2** for a second holly leaf. Attach holly leaves to the cup of milk.

BERRY

Rnd 1: with **red** yarn, sc 5 in magic loop [5]

Rnd 2: 2 sc in each st around [10]

Rnd 3: sc in each st around [10]

Rnd 4: (sc2tog) repeat 5 times [5]

Stuff with fiberfill. Fasten off and leave a long yarn tail. With yarn needle weave the tail through FLO to close opening, weave in ends.

Attach berry to the holly leaves.

CHOCOLATE CHIP COOKIES (MAKE 3)

Rnd 1: with **tan** yarn, sc 8 in magic loop [8]

Rnd 2: 2 sc in each st around [16]

Rnd 3: (sc 1, 2 sc in next st) repeat 6 times [24]

Rnd 4: (sc 2, 2 sc in next st) repeat 6 times [32]

Rnd 5: (sc 3, 2 sc in next st) repeat 6 times [40]

Rnd 6: (sc 4, 2 sc in next st) repeat 6 times [48]

Invisible fasten off and weave in ends.

Place 7mm safety eyes between **Rnds 2 and 3** with 5 sts in between. With yarn needle and **brown** yarn, add stitches for the chocolate chips.

Leaf chart

Add stitches for mouth and cheeks using **black** and **brown** yarn (see Making Up: Stitching Facial Details).

Repeat **Rnds 1–6** for the back of the cookie. Do not fasten off the second piece. With a yarn needle and **brown** yarn, add stitches for the chocolate chips.

Rnd 7: place the front and back pieces of the cookie together, stuff lightly with fiberfill, sl st in each st around to join them together [48]

Fasten off and weave in ends.

Repeat **Rnds 1–7** two more times for a total of three chocolate chip cookies.

POINSETTIA

CHRISTMAS ON POINT!

Materials

- 3.5mm (E/4) and 2.75mm (C/2) crochet hooks
- Paintbox Yarns Cotton Aran yarn: one 50g (1¾oz) ball each of Vanilla Cream (**cream**) and Soft Fudge (**brown**)
- Paintbox Yarns Cotton DK yarn: one 50g (1¾oz) ball each of Pillar Red (**red**), Racing Green (**dark green**), and Buttercup Yellow (**yellow**)
- Scraps of **black** and **red** yarn
- 7mm safety eyes
- Fiberfill stuffing
- Yarn needle
- Stitch marker

Finished Size

10cm (4in) tall by 7.5cm (3in) wide

Gauge

5 sc sts and 6 rows = 2.5cm (1in) using Aran yarn

6 sc sts and 7 rows = 2.5cm (1in) using DK yarn

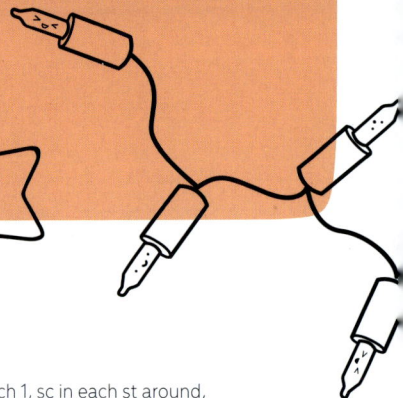

POT

Rnd 1: with **3.5mm** hook and **cream Aran** yarn, sc 6 in magic loop [6]

Rnd 2: 2 sc in each st around [12]

Rnd 3: (sc 1, 2 sc in next st) 6 times [18]

Rnd 4: (sc 2, 2 sc in next st) 6 times [24]

Rnd 5: (sc 3, 2 sc in next st) 6 times [30]

Rnd 6: (sc 4, 2 sc in next st) 6 times [36]

Rnd 7: working in BLO, sc in each st around [36]

Rnds 8–11: sc in each st around [36]

Rnd 12: (sc 5, 2 sc in next st) 6 times [42]

Rnds 13–15: sc in each st around [42]

Place 7mm safety eyes between **Rnds 11 and 12**, with 4 sts in between. Begin to stuff with fiberfill. Do not fasten off and cut yarn. Make the dirt before moving on to **Rnd 16**.

Rnd 16: place the dirt in the pot and line up the stitches from **Rnd 15** of the pot and **Rnd 7** of the dirt. With the yarn used to make the pot, sc in each st around, working in both loops of both pieces to join them together (see Making Up: Crocheting Two Pieces Together) [42]

Rnd 17: ch 1, sc in each st around, join with sl st in first st [42]

Rnd 18: sl st in each st around [42]

Invisible fasten off (see Finishing: Invisible Fasten Off) and weave in ends. Add stitches for the mouth and cheeks using **black** and **red** yarn (see Making Up: Stitching Facial Details). With **cream Aran** yarn, begin shaping by inserting needle from center bottom to center top, then take needle back down from center top to slightly off-center bottom and back up to center top. Pull to create an indentation in the bottom of the pot (see Making Up: Shaping). Fasten off and weave in ends.

DIRT

Rnd 1: with **3.5mm** hook and **brown Aran** yarn, sc 6 in magic loop [6]

Rnd 2: 2 sc in each st around [12]

Rnd 3: (sc 1, 2 sc in next st) 6 times [18]

Rnd 4: (sc 2, 2 sc in next st) 6 times [24]

Rnd 5: (sc 3, 2 sc in next st) 6 times [30]

Rnd 6: (sc 4, 2 sc in next st) 6 times [36]

Rnd 7: (sc 5, 2 sc in next st) 6 times [42]

Invisible fasten off and weave in ends.

SMALL PETALS (MAKE 6)

Rnd 1: with **2.75mm** hook and **red DK** yarn, sc 4 in magic loop [4]

Rnd 2: (sc 1, 2 sc in next st) 2 times [6]

Rnd 3: (sc 2, 2 sc in next st) 2 times [8]

Rnd 4: (sc 3, 2 sc in next st) 2 times [10]

Rnd 5: (sc 4, 2 sc in next st) 2 times [12]

Rnds 6–7: sc in each st around [12]

Rnd 8: (sc2tog, sc 4) 2 times [10]

Rnd 9: (sc2tog, sc 3) 2 times [8]

Sl st in next st. Fasten off, leaving a long tail. Do not stuff with fiberfill. Flatten and sew opening closed with a yarn needle and yarn tail, then sew the two sides together at the bottom of the petal. Using a yarn tail from one of the petals, sew all six petals together in a circle (1).

CENTER

Rnd 1: with **2.75mm** hook and **yellow DK** yarn, sc 6 in magic loop [6]

Rnd 2: working in FLO, 5 sc in each st around [30]

Rnd 3: working in BLO from **Rnd 1**, (2 sc + ch 2 + 2 sc in next st) 6 times [36]

Fasten off and weave in ends.

LARGE PETALS (MAKE 4 RED AND 2 GREEN)

Rnd 1: with **2.75mm** hook and **DK** yarn in the appropriate color, sc 4 in magic loop [4]

Rnd 2: (sc 1, 2 sc in next st) 2 times [6]

Rnd 3: (sc 2, 2 sc in next st) 2 times [8]

Rnd 4: (sc 3, 2 sc in next st) 2 times [10]

Rnd 5: (sc 4, 2 sc in next st) 2 times [12]

Rnd 6: (sc 5, 2 sc in next st) 2 times [14]

Rnds 7–8: sc in each st around [14]

Rnd 9: (sc2tog, sc 5) 2 times [12]

Rnd 10: (sc2tog, sc 4) 2 times [10]

Rnd 11: (sc2tog, sc 3) 2 times [8]

Sl st in next st. Fasten off, leaving a long tail. Do not stuff with fiberfill. Flatten and sew opening closed with a yarn needle and yarn tail, then sew the two sides together at the bottom of the petal. Make a total of six petals—four with **red** yarn and two with **dark green** yarn.

Using a yarn tail from one of the petals, sew all six petals together in a circle (2).

Attach the circle of large petals to the dirt.

Attach the circle of small petals to the top of the large petals.

Attach the center to the circle of small petals (3).

ORANGE

ORANGE YOU GLAD IT'S CHRISTMAS?

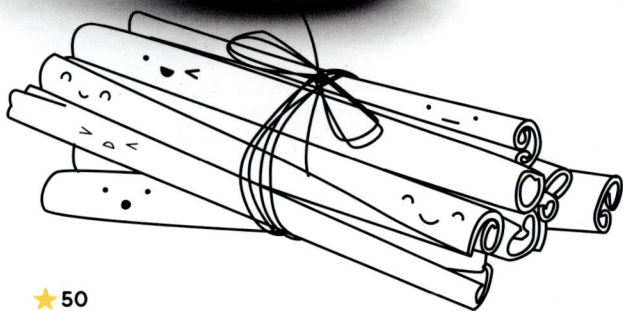

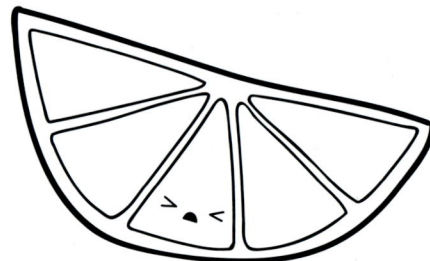

Materials

- 3.5mm (E/4) crochet hook
- Yarn And Colors Epic Aran: one 50g (1¾oz) ball each of Cantaloupe (**orange**) and Peony Leaf (**green**)
- 9mm safety eyes
- Scraps of **black** and **pink** yarn
- Fiberfill stuffing
- Yarn needle
- Stitch marker

Finished Size

9cm (3½in) tall by 9cm (3½in) wide

Gauge

5 sc sts and 6 rows = 2.5cm (1in)

ORANGE

Rnd 1: with **green** yarn, sc 6 in magic loop [6]

Rnd 2: change to **orange** yarn, 2 sc in each st around [12]

Rnd 3: (sc 1, 2 sc in next st) repeat 6 times [18]

Rnd 4: (sc 2, 2 sc in next st) repeat 6 times [24]

Rnd 5: (sc 3, 2 sc in next st) repeat 6 times [30]

Rnd 6: (sc 4, 2 sc in next st) repeat 6 times [36]

Rnd 7: sc in each st around [36]

Rnd 8: (sc 5, 2 sc in next st) repeat 6 times [42]

Rnd 9: sc in each st around [42]

Rnd 10: (sc 6, 2 sc in next st) repeat 6 times [48]

Rnd 11: sc in each st around [48]

Rnd 12: (sc 7, 2 sc in next st) repeat 6 times [54]

Rnd 13: sc in each st around [54]

Rnd 14: (sc 7, sc2tog) repeat 6 times [48]

Rnds 15–16: sc in each st around [48]

Rnd 17: (sc 6, sc2tog) repeat 6 times [42]

Rnds 18–19: sc in each st around [42]

Place 9mm safety eyes between **Rnds 13 and 14** with 6 sts in between. Begin to stuff with fiberfill.

Rnd 20: (sc 5, sc2tog) repeat 6 times [36]

Rnd 21: (sc 4, sc2tog) repeat 6 times [30]

Rnd 22: (sc 3, sc2tog) repeat 6 times [24]

Rnd 23: (sc 2, sc2tog) repeat 6 times [18]

Rnd 24: (sc 1, sc2tog) repeat 6 times [12]

Rnd 25: (sc2tog) repeat 6 times [6]

Finish stuffing. Fasten off and leave a long yarn tail. With a yarn needle weave the tail through FLO to close opening, weave in ends.

Stitch the mouth and cheeks using **black** and **pink** yarn (see Making Up: Stitching Facial Details).

LEAVES (MAKE 2)

Rnd 1: with **green** yarn, ch 10, sl st in 2nd ch from hook, sc 1, hdc 1, dc 4, hdc 1, sc 3 in last st, working on the other side of the foundation ch, hdc 1, dc 4, hdc 1, sc 1, sl st in beginning skipped ch st [19]

Invisible fasten off (see Finishing: Invisible Fasten Off) and weave in all ends. Attach the leaves to the top of the orange.

Leaf chart

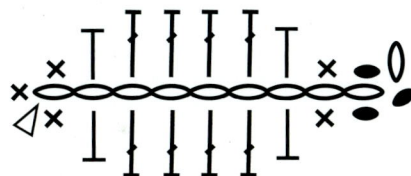

The tradition of giving Christmas oranges began in 19th-century Europe, where an orange was a rare privilege and a traditional gift among families with few means. Oranges are also a symbol of gold and are placed in children's stockings as a reimagined bag of gold left by St Nicholas.

MISTLETOE

I CAN FEEL THE CHRISTMAS SPIRIT FROM MY HEAD TO MY MISTLETOES!

Materials

- 2.75mm (C/2) crochet hook
- Paintbox Yarns Cotton DK yarn: one 50g (1¾oz) ball each of Red Wine (**red**), Spearmint Green (**green**), and Paper White (**white**)
- 6mm safety eyes
- Scrap of **black** yarn
- Fiberfill stuffing
- Yarn needle
- Stitch marker

Finished Size

20cm (8in) tall by 12.5cm (5in) wide

Gauge

6 sc sts and 7 rows = 2.5cm (1in)

FOUR-LEAF MISTLETOE (MAKE 2)

Note: On **Rnd 1** and **Rnds 3–5** you will be making a leaf. **Row 2** you will be making the stem.

With **green** yarn, ch 12

Rnd 1: sc in 2nd ch from hook, sc 1, hdc 2, dc 4, hdc 2, sc 3, working on the other side of the foundation ch, hdc 2, dc 4, hdc 2, sc 2, sl st in beginning skipped ch st [24] (1 leaf made)

Row 2: ch 31, working in back bump loops, sl st in 2nd ch from hook, sl st 29 [30]

Rnd 3: make leaf as **Rnd 1**

Invisible fasten off (see Finishing: Invisible Fasten Off) and weave in all ends.

Rnd 4: join **green** yarn in ch 10 from Row 2, then make leaf as **Rnd 1**

Invisible fasten off and weave in all ends.

Rnd 5: join **green** yarn in ch 10 from **Row 2**, opposite the other leaf, then make leaf as **Rnd 1**

Invisible fasten off and weave in all ends.

Repeat **Rnd 1**, **Row 2** and **Rnds 3–5** for a second four-leaf mistletoe (1).

SIX-LEAF MISTLETOE (MAKE 2)

Note: On **Rnd 1** and **Rnds 3–7** you will be making a leaf. **Row 2** you will be making the stem.

With **green** yarn, ch 12

Rnd 1: sc in 2nd ch from hook, sc 1, hdc 2, dc 4, hdc 2, sc 3 in last ch, working on the other side of the foundation ch, hdc 2, dc 4, hdc 2, sc 2, sl st in beginning skipped ch st [24] (1 leaf made)

Row 2: ch 41, working in back bump loops (see Special Stitches), sl st in 2nd ch from hook, sl st 29 [40]

Rnd 3: make leaf as **Rnd 1**

Invisible fasten off and weave in all ends.

Rnd 4: join **green** yarn in ch 10 from **Row 2**, then make leaf as **Rnd 1**

Invisible fasten off and weave in all ends.

Rnd 5: join **green** yarn in ch 10 from **Row 2**, opposite other leaf, then make leaf as **Rnd 1**

Invisible fasten off and weave in all ends.

Rnd 6: join **green** yarn in ch 20 from **Row 2**, then make leaf as **Rnd 1**

Invisible fasten off and weave in all ends.

Rnd 7: join **green** yarn in ch 20 from **Row 2**, opposite other leaf, then make leaf as **Rnd 1**

Invisible fasten off and weave in all ends.

Repeat **Rnd 1**, **Row 2** and **Rnds 3–7** for a second six-leaf mistletoe (2).

BERRIES (MAKE 7)

Rnd 1: with **white** yarn, sc 5 in magic loop [5]

Rnd 2: 2 sc in each st around [10]

Rnd 3: sc in each st around [10]

Rnd 4: (sc2tog) repeat 5 times [5]

Stuff with fiberfill. Fasten off and leave a long yarn tail. With yarn needle weave tail through FLO to close opening, weave in ends.

Repeat **Rnds 1–4** for a total of seven white berries. Attach them to the mistletoe with one or two berries on each stem.

BOW

With **red** yarn, ch 54

Row 1: sc in 2nd ch from hook, sc 52, turn [53]

Rows 2–12: ch 1, sc 53, turn [53]

Fasten off and leave a long yarn tail.

With yarn tail, sew the two ends together. Scrunch the bow in the middle and with a piece of yarn, wrap the center of the bow a couple of times and tie a knot to secure.

BOW TAILS

With **red** yarn, ch 7

Row 1: sc in 2nd ch form hook, sc 5, turn [6]

Rows 2–36: ch 1, sc 6, turn [6]

Fasten off and weave in ends. Fold the bow tail in half and attach to the back of the bow.

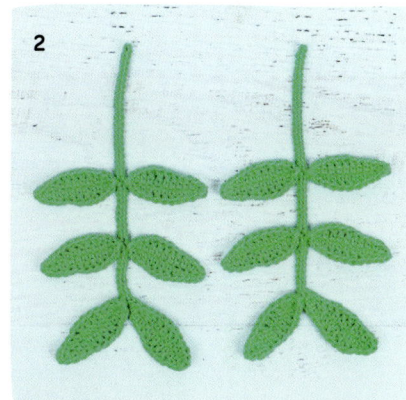

CENTER OF BOW

With **red** yarn, ch 8

Row 1: sc in 2nd ch form hook, sc 6, turn [7]

Rows 2–21: ch 1, sc 7, turn [7]

Fasten off and leave a long yarn tail.

Place 6mm safety eyes between **Rows 12 and 13** with 4 sts in between.

Stitch the mouth using **black** yarn (see Making Up: Stitching Facial Details).

Wrap the bow center around the middle of the bow. With the yarn tail, sew the two ends of the center piece together (3).

Attach all four stems ofmistletoe to the back of the bow.

BACK BOW PIECE

With **red** yarn, ch 7

Row 1: sc in 2nd ch form hook, sc 5, turn [6]

Rows 2–6: ch 1, sc 6, turn [6]

Fasten off and weave in ends. Attach to the back of the bow, over the mistletoe stems.

Add a hanging loop using **red** yarn (see Making Up: Ornament Hanging Loop).

SWEETS

WILL YOU BE MY SWEETIE?

Materials

- 2.75mm (C/2) crochet hook
- Paintbox Yarns Cotton DK yarn: one 50g (1¾oz) ball each of Red Wine (**red**), Melon Sorbet (**yellow**), Lime Green (**lime green**), Dolphin Blue (**blue**), and Bubblegum Pink (**pink**)
- 7mm safety eyes
- Scraps of **black** and **pink** yarn
- Fiberfill stuffing
- Yarn needle
- Stitch marker

Finished Size

7.5cm (3in) long by 4.5cm (1¾in) wide

Gauge

6 sc sts and 7 rows = 2.5cm (1in)

SWEET (MAKE 1 IN EACH COLOR)

Rnd 1: with your choice of yarn color, sc 6 in magic loop [6]

Rnd 2: 2 sc in each st around [12]

Rnd 3: working in BLO, (sc 1, 2 sc in next st) repeat 6 times [18]

Rnd 4: (sc 2, 2 sc in next st) repeat 6 times [24]

Rnd 5: (sc 3, 2 sc in next st) repeat 6 times [30]

Rnds 6–10: sc in each st around [30]

Rnd 11: (sc 3, sc2tog) repeat 6 times [24]

Place 7mm safety eyes between **Rnds 5 and 6** and also between **Rnds 10 and 11**.

Begin to stuff with fiberfill.

Rnd 12: (sc 2, sc2tog) repeat 6 times [18]

Rnd 13: (sc 1, sc2tog) repeat 6 times [12]

Rnd 14: working in BLO, (sc2tog) repeat 6 times [6]

Fasten off and leave a long yarn tail. With a yarn needle, weave the tail through FLO to close the opening. Fasten off and weave in ends.

WRAPPER

Join matching yarn in FLO of **Rnd 2** of sweet (1).

Rnd 1: ch 1, sc in each st around, sl st in first sc st to join rnd [12] (2)

Rnd 2: ch 3, 2 dc in each st around, sl st in first dc st to join rnd [24]

Rnd 3: (sc 1, sc2tog) repeat 8 times [16] (3)

Invisible fasten off (see Finishing: Invisible Fasten Off) and weave in ends (4).

Join matching yarn in front loop of **Rnd 13** of sweet. Repeat **Rnds 1–3** for the second wrapper.

Invisible fasten off and weave in ends. Add stitches for the mouth and cheeks using **black** and **pink** yarn (see Making Up: Stitching Facial Details).

Trees adorned with sugary decorations have been a visual feast for centuries, and did you know, over 90 percent of people give chocolate and candy as gifts during the holidays? Candy certainly plays an important role at Christmas.

DRUM

MY HEART ONLY BEATS FOR YOU!

Materials

- 3.5mm (E/4) and 2.75mm (C/2) crochet hooks
- Paintbox Yarns Cotton Aran yarn: one 50g (1¾oz) ball each of Champagne White (**white**), Red Wine (**red**), and Glorious Gold (**gold**)
- Paintbox Yarns Cotton DK yarn: one 50g (1¾oz) ball of Coffee Bean (**dark brown**)
- Anchor Metallic Gold thread in color 303 (**metallic gold**)
- 8mm safety eyes
- Scraps of **black** and **gold** yarn
- Fiberfill stuffing
- Yarn needle
- Stitch marker

Finished Size

7.5cm (3in) tall (including drumsticks) by 7.5cm (3in) wide

Gauge

5 sc sts and 6 rows = 2.5cm (1in) using Aran yarn

DRUM

Rnd 1: with **3.5mm** hook and **white Aran** yarn, sc 6 in magic loop [6]

Rnd 2: 2 sc in each st around [12]

Rnd 3: (sc 1, 2 sc in next st) repeat 6 times [18]

Rnd 4: (sc 2, 2 sc in next st) repeat 6 times [24]

Rnd 5: (sc 3, 2 sc in next st) repeat 6 times [30]

Rnd 6: (sc 4, 2 sc in next st) repeat 6 times [36]

Rnd 7: change to **gold Aran** yarn, (sc 5, 2 sc in next st) repeat 6 times [42]

Rnd 8: working in BLO, sc in each st around [42]

Rnd 9: sc in each st around [42]

Rnd 10: change to **red Aran** yarn, working in BLO, sc in each st around [42]

Rnds 11–16: sc in each st around [42]

Place 8mm safety eyes between **Rnds 12 and 13** with 5 sts in between, begin to stuff with fiberfill.

Rnd 17: change to **gold Aran** yarn, sl st in each st around [42]

Rnd 18: working in BLO, sc in each st around [42]

Rnd 19: sc in each st around [42]

Rnd 20: change to **white Aran** yarn, working in BLO, (sc 5, sc2tog) repeat 6 times [36]

Rnd 21: (sc 4, sc2tog) repeat 6 times [30]

Rnd 22: (sc 3, sc2tog) repeat 6 times [24]

Rnd 23: (sc 2, sc2tog) repeat 6 times [18]

Rnd 24: (sc 1, sc2tog) repeat 6 times [12]

Rnd 25: (sc2tog) repeat 6 times [6]

Finish stuffing with fiberfill. Fasten off and leave a long yarn tail. With a yarn needle weave the tail through FLO to close opening, weave in ends.

Stitch the mouth and cheeks using **black** and **gold** yarn (see Making Up: Stitching Facial Details).

Begin shaping by inserting needle threaded with **white Aran** yarn from center bottom to center top, insert needle back down from center top to slightly off-center bottom. Insert needle from center bottom to center top. Pull to create an indentation in the bottom of the drum (see Making Up: Shaping). Fasten off and weave in ends.

With **metallic gold** thread and a yarn needle, work in the FLO in **Rnds 9 and 17** to create the triangular yarn decoration on the drum. Skip every 5 sts when working in and out of the front loops.

Rnd 26: join **gold Aran** yarn in FLO of **Rnd 7**, sl st in each st around [42]

Fasten off and weave in ends.

Rnd 27: join **gold Aran** yarn in FLO of **Rnd 19**, sl st in each st around [42]

Fasten off and weave in ends.

DRUMSTICKS (MAKE 2)

Rnd 1: with **2.75mm** hook and **dark brown DK** yarn sc 6 in magic loop [6]

Rnd 2: (sc 1, 2 sc in next st) repeat 3 times [9]

Rnds 3–4: sc in each st around [9]

Rnd 5: (sc 1, sc2tog) repeat 3 times [6]

Rnds 6–11: sc in each st around [6]

Stuff with fiberfill. Fasten off and leave a long yarn tail. With a yarn needle weave the tail through FLO to close opening, weave in ends.

Repeat **Rnds 1–11** for a second drumstick. Attach both to the top of the drum.

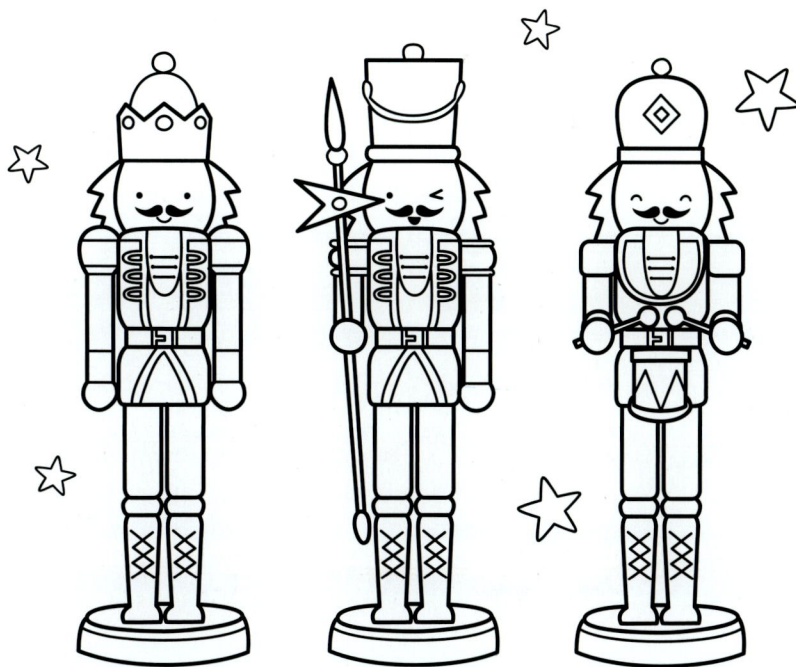

FRUIT CAKE

YOU'D BETTER
BE GOOD
FOR GOODNESS' CAKE!

Materials

- 3.5mm (E/4) and 2.75mm (C/2) crochet hooks
- Paintbox Yarns Cotton Aran yarn: one 50g (1¾oz) ball each of Soft Fudge (**brown**), Red Wine (**red**), Spearmint Green (**green**), and Champagne White (**white**)
- Paintbox Yarns Cotton DK yarn: one 50g (1¾oz) ball each of Spearmint Green (**green**), Pillar Red (**red**), and Soft Fudge (**brown**)
- 7mm safety eyes
- Scraps of **black** and **red** yarn
- Fiberfill stuffing
- Yarn needle
- Stitch marker

Finished Size

7.5cm (3in) tall by 7.5cm (3in) wide

Gauge

5 sc sts and 6 rows = 2.5cm (1in) using Aran yarn

CAKE

Rnd 1: with **3.5mm** hook and **brown Aran** yarn sc 6 in magic loop [6]

Rnd 2: 2 sc in each st around [12]

Rnd 3: (sc 1, 2 sc in next st) repeat 6 times [18]

Rnd 4: (sc 2, 2 sc in next st) repeat 6 times [24]

Rnd 5: (sc 3, 2 sc in next st) repeat 6 times [30]

Rnd 6: (sc 4, 2 sc in next st) repeat 6 times [36]

Rnd 7: (sc 5, 2 sc in next st) repeat 6 times [42]

Rnd 8: working in BLO, sc in each st around [42]

Rnds 9–10: sc in each st around [42]

Rnd 11: (change to **green Aran** yarn, sc 3, change to **red Aran** yarn sc 3) repeat 7 times [42]

Rnd 12: change to **brown Aran** yarn, sc in each st around [42]

Rnds 13–14: sc in each st around [42]

Rnd 15: (change to **red Aran** yarn, sc 3, change to **green Aran** yarn sc 3) repeat 7 times [42]

Rnd 16: change to **brown Aran** yarn, sc in each st around [42]

Rnds 17–18: sc in each st around [42]

Place 7mm safety eyes between **Rnds 12 and 13** with 4 sts in between. Begin to stuff with fiberfill.

Rnd 19: working in BLO, (sc 5, sc2tog) repeat 6 times [36]

Rnd 20: (sc 4, sc2tog) repeat 6 times [30]

Rnd 21: (sc 3, sc2tog) repeat 6 times [24]

Rnd 22: (sc 2, sc2tog) repeat 6 times [18]

Rnd 23: (sc 1, sc2tog) repeat 6 times [12]

Rnd 24: (sc2tog) repeat 6 times [6]

Finish stuffing with fiberfill. Fasten off and leave a long yarn tail. With a yarn needle weave the tail through FLO to close opening, weave in ends (see Making Up: Closing Stitches Through Front Loops).

Stitch the mouth and cheeks using **black** and **red** yarn (see Making Up: Stitching Facial Details).

Begin shaping by inserting a needle threaded with **brown Aran** yarn from center bottom to center top, insert the needle back down from center top to slightly off-center bottom. Insert needle from center bottom to center top. Pull to create an indentation in the bottom of the cake (see Making Up: Shaping). Fasten off and weave in ends.

ICING

Rnd 1: with **3.5mm** hook and **white Aran** yarn, sc 6 in magic loop [6]

Rnd 2: 2 sc in each st around [12]

Rnd 3: (sc 1, 2 sc in next st) repeat 6 times [18]

Rnd 4: (sc 2, 2 sc in next st) repeat 6 times [24]

Rnd 5: (sc 3, 2 sc in next st) repeat 6 times [30]

Rnd 6: (sc 4, 2 sc in next st) repeat 6 times [36]

Rnd 7: (sc 5, 2 sc in next st) repeat 6 times [42]

Rnd 8: (sc 1, hdc 1, dc 1, tr 1, dc 1, hdc 1, sc 1, hdc 1, dc 1, tr 1, 2 tr in next st, tr 1, dc 1, hdc 1) repeat 3 times [45]

Invisible fasten off (see Finishing: Invisible Fasten Off) and weave in all ends. Attach to the top of the cake.

PECANS (MAKE 4)

Rnd 1: with **2.75mm** hook and **brown DK** yarn, ch 8, hdc in 3rd ch from hook, hdc 4, 3 hdc in last ch st, working on the other side of the foundation ch, hdc 4, 2 hdc in last st [14]

Rnd 2: working in BLO in **Rnd 1**, sl st 2, sc 3, sl st 4, sc 3, sl st 2 [14]

Rnd 3: working in FLO in **Rnd 1**, sl st 2, sc 3, sl st 4, sc 3, sl st 2 [14]

Rnd 4: working down the center in between the sts in **Rnd 1**, sl st 1, sc 3, sl st 1 [5]

Fasten off and weave in ends. Repeat **Rnds 1–4** for a total of 4 pecans. Attach pecans to the top of the icing in a pattern.

CANDIED FRUIT (MAKE 2 RED AND 3 GREEN)

Rnd 1: with **2.75mm** hook and **red/ green DK** yarn, sc 6 in magic loop [6]

Rnd 2: 2 sc in each st around [12]

Rnd 3: sc in each st around [12]

Rnd 4: (sc2tog) repeat 6 times [6]

Stuff with fiberfill. Fasten off and leave a long yarn tail. With a yarn needle weave the tail through FLO to close opening, weave in ends.

Repeat **Rnds 1–4** for a total of two red candied fruit and three green candied fruit. Attach them to the top of the icing in between the pecans.

Fruit cake can be traced to ancient Egypt, where delicious and long-lasting cakes were placed in the great pyramids with deceased royal dignitaries to sweeten their experience in the afterlife.

SNOWMAN

THERE'S SNOW PLACE LIKE HOME FOR THE HOLIDAYS

Materials

- 3.5mm (E/4) crochet hook
- Paintbox Yarns Cotton Aran yarn: one 50g (1¾oz) ball each of Paper White (**white**), Grass Green (**green**), Red Wine (**red**), Pure Black (**black**), and Blood Orange (**orange**)
- 7mm safety eyes
- Fiberfill stuffing
- Yarn needle
- Stitch marker

Finished Size

11.5cm (4½in) tall by 6.5cm (2½in) wide

Gauge

5 sc sts and 6 rows = 2.5cm (1in)

SNOWMAN

Rnd 1: with **white** yarn, sc 10 in magic loop [10]

Rnd 2: (sc 1, 2 sc in next st) repeat 5 times [15]

Rnd 3: (sc 2, 2 sc in next st) repeat 5 times [20]

Rnd 4: (sc 3, 2 sc in next st) repeat 5 times [25]

Rnd 5: (sc 4, 2 sc in next st) repeat 5 times [30]

Rnds 6–10: sc in each st around [30]

Rnd 11: (sc 4, sc2tog) repeat 5 times [25]

Rnd 12: sc in each st around [25]

Rnd 13: (sc 3, sc2tog) repeat 5 times [20]

Rnd 14: (sc 2, sc2tog) repeat 5 times [15]

Rnd 15: (sc 2, 2 sc in next st) repeat 5 times [20]

Rnd 16: (sc 3, 2 sc in next st) repeat 5 times [25]

Rnds 17–19: sc in each st around [25]

Place 7mm safety eyes between **Rnds 17 and 18** with 2 sts in between. Begin to stuff with fiberfill.

Rnd 20: (sc 3, sc2tog) repeat 5 times [20]

Rnd 21: (sc 2, sc2tog) repeat 5 times [15]

Rnd 22: (sc, sc2tog) repeat 5 times [10]

Rnd 23: (sc2tog) repeat 5 times [5]

Fasten off and leave a long yarn tail. With a yarn needle, weave the tail through FLO to close the opening. Fasten off and weave in ends.

NOSE

Rnd 1: with **orange** yarn, ch 3, sl st in 2nd ch from hook, sc in last ch st [2]

Fasten off and weave in ends. Attach to the snowman.

TOP HAT

Rnd 1: with **black** yarn, sc 10 in magic loop [10]

Rnd 2: (sc 1, 2 sc in next st) repeat 5 times [15]

Rnd 3: working in BLO, sc in each st around [15]

Rnd 4: (sc 3, sc2tog) repeat 3 times [12]

Rnds 5–6: sc in each st around [12]

Rnd 7: working in FLO, sc in each st around [12]

Rnd 8: 2 sc in each st around [24]

Fasten off and weave in ends. Stuff with fiberfill and attach to the top of the snowman.

SCARF

With **green** yarn, ch 3

Row 1: sc in 2nd ch from hook, sc 1, turn [2]

Rows 2–4: ch 1, sc 2, turn [2]

Row 5: change to **red** yarn, ch 1, sc 2, turn [2]

Rows 6–8: ch 1, sc 2, turn [2]

Rows 9–52: repeat **Rows 5–8**, alternating between **green** and **red** yarn

Fasten off and weave in ends. With small pieces of **green** yarn, tie two yarn tassels to each end of the scarf. Tie the scarf around the neck of the snowman.

Want to make your snowman smaller? Simply use 6mm safety eyes, a 2.75mm (C/2) crochet hook, and DK weight yarn. The finished snowman will measure 9cm (3½in) tall by 4cm (1½in) wide.

MINCE PIE

I ONLY HAVE PIES FOR YOU!

Materials

- 3.5mm (E/4) crochet hook
- Paintbox Yarns Cotton Aran yarn: one 50g (1¾oz) ball each of Light Caramel (**tan**) and Soft Fudge (**dark brown**)
- 7mm safety eyes
- Scraps of **black** and **dark brown** yarn
- Fiberfill stuffing
- Yarn needle
- Stitch marker

Finished Size

4cm (1½in) tall by 10cm (4in) wide

Gauge

5 sc sts and 6 rows = 2.5cm (1in)

FILLING

Rnd 1: with **dark brown** yarn, sc 6 in magic loop [6]

Rnd 2: 2 sc in each st around [12]

Rnd 3: (sc 1, 2 sc in next st) repeat 6 times [18]

Rnd 4: (sc 2, 2 sc in next st) repeat 6 times [24]

Rnd 5: (sc 3, 2 sc in next st) repeat 6 times [30]

Rnd 6: (sc 4, 2 sc in next st) repeat 6 times [36]

Rnd 7: (sc 5, 2 sc in next st) repeat 5 times, (sc 1, 2 sc in next st) repeat 3 times [44]

Invisible fasten off (see Finishing: Invisible Fasten Off) and weave in ends.

PIE CRUST

Rnd 1: with **tan** yarn, sc 6 in magic loop [6]

Rnd 2: 2 sc in each st around [12]

Rnd 3: (sc 1, 2 sc in next st) repeat 6 times [18]

Rnd 4: (sc 2, 2 sc in next st) repeat 6 times [24]

Rnd 5: (sc 3, 2 sc in next st) repeat 6 times [30]

Rnd 6: working in BLO, sc in each st around [30]

Rnd 7: (sc 4, 2 sc in next st) repeat 6 times [36]

Rnd 8: sc in each st around [36]

Rnd 9: (sc 5, 2 sc in next st) repeat 6 times [42]

Rnd 10: (sc 20, 2 sc in next st) repeat 2 times [44]

Rnd 11: sc in each st around [44]

Place 7mm safety eyes between **Rnds 9 and 10** with 4 sts in between, begin to stuff with fiberfill.

Do not fasten off.

Rnd 12: Place the filling in the pie crust and line up the stitches from **Rnd 11** of the pie crust and **Rnd 7** of the filling. With the yarn used to make the pie crust, sc in each st around working in both loops of both pieces to join them together [44]

Rnd 13: (skip next st, 3 dc in next st, skip next st, sl st 1) repeat 11 times [44]

Fasten off and weave in ends.

Begin shaping by inserting a needle threaded with **tan** yarn from center bottom to center top, insert needle back down from center top to slightly off-center bottom. Insert needle from center bottom to center top. Pull to create an indentation in the bottom of the Pie (see Making Up: Shaping). Fasten off and weave in ends.

Add stitches for mouth and cheeks using **black** and **dark brown** yarn (see Making Up: Stitching Facial Details).

STAR

Rnd 1: with **tan** yarn, in magic loop, ch 2, dc 1 (ch 1, 2 dc) repeat 4 times, ch 1, sl st in beginning ch 2 [15]

Rnd 2: (ch 4, sc in 2nd ch from hook, hdc in next ch, dc in last ch, sl st in ch-1 space) repeat 5 times [20]

Fasten off and weave in ends. Attach the star to the top of the mince pie.

HOT COCOA

WAKE ME UP BEFORE YOU COCOA...

COCOA

Rnd 1: with **3.5mm** hook and **brown Aran** yarn, sc 6 in magic loop [6]

Rnd 2: 2 sc in each st around [12]

Rnd 3: (sc 1, 2 sc in next st) repeat 6 times [18]

Rnd 4: (sc 2, 2 sc in next st) repeat 6 times [24]

Rnd 5: (sc 3, 2 sc in next st) repeat 6 times [30]

Rnd 6: (sc 4, 2 sc in next st) repeat 6 times [36]

Invisible fasten off (see Finishing: Invisible Fasten Off) and weave in ends.

MUG

Rnd 1: with **3.5mm** hook and **red Aran** yarn, sc 6 in magic loop [6]

Rnd 2: 2 sc in each st around [12]

Rnd 3: (sc 1, 2 sc in next st) repeat 6 times [18]

Rnd 4: (sc 2, 2 sc in next st) repeat 6 times [24]

Rnd 5: (sc 3, 2 sc in next st) repeat 6 times [30]

Rnd 6: (sc 4, 2 sc in next st) repeat 6 times [36]

Rnd 7: working in BLO, sc in each st around [36]

Rnds 8–19: sc in each st around [36]

Do not fasten off and cut yarn. Place 8mm safety eyes between **Rnds 13 and 14** with 4 sts in between. Begin to stuff with fiberfill.

Rnd 20: Place the cocoa in the mug and line up the stitches from **Rnd 19** of the mug with **Rnd 6** of the cocoa. With the yarn used to make the mug, sc in each st around working in both loops of both pieces to join them together [36]

Rnd 21: sl st in each st around [36]

Invisible fasten off and weave in ends.

Stitch the mouth and cheeks using **black** and **pink** yarn (see Making Up: Stitching Facial Details).

Begin shaping (see Making Up: Shaping) by inserting a needle, threaded with **red Aran** yarn, from center bottom to center top, insert needle back down from center top to slightly off-center bottom. Insert needle from center bottom to center top. Pull to create an indentation in the bottom of the mug.

Fasten off and weave in ends.

HANDLE

Rnd 1: with **3.5mm** hook and **red Aran** yarn, sc 5 in magic loop [5]

Rnds 2–18: sc in each st around [5]

Do not stuff with fiberfill. Fasten off and leave a long yarn tail. With a yarn needle, weave the tail through FLO to close the opening. Fasten off and weave in ends.

Attach to the side of the mug.

MARSHMALLOWS (MAKE 3)

Rnd 1: with **2.75mm** hook and **white DK** yarn, sc 5 in magic loop [5]

Rnd 2: 2 sc in each st around [10]

Rnd 3: (sc 1, 2 sc in next st) repeat 5 times [15]

Rnd 4: working in BLO, sc in each st around [15]

Rnds 5–9: sc in each st around [15]

Place 5mm safety eyes between **Rnds 6 and 7** with 2 sts in between. Begin to stuff with fiberfill.

Rnd 10: (working in BLO, sc 1, sc2tog) repeat 5 times [10]

Rnd 11: (sc2tog) repeat 5 times [5]

Fasten off and leave a long yarn tail. With a yarn needle, weave the tail through FLO to close the opening. Fasten off and weave in ends.

Stitch the mouth and cheeks using **black** and **pink** yarn.

Make a total of three marshmallows. Attach the marshmallows to the top of the cocoa.

BALLERINA

Materials

- 2.75mm (C/2) crochet hook
- Paintbox Yarns Cotton DK yarn: one 50g (1¾oz) ball each of Light Caramel (**tan**), Blush Pink (**light pink**), Ballet Pink (**dark pink**), and Soft Fudge (**brown**)
- 6mm safety eyes
- Scraps of **tan** and **pink** yarn
- Fiberfill stuffing
- Yarn needle
- Stitch marker

Finished Size

19cm (7½in) tall by 7.5cm (3in) wide

Gauge

6 sc sts and 7 rows = 2.5cm (1in)

BODY AND HEAD

Rnd 1: with **light pink** yarn, sc 6 in magic loop [6]

Rnd 2: (sc 1, 2 sc in next st) repeat 3 times [9]

Rnds 3–6: sc in each st around [6]

Rnd 7: change to **tan** yarn, working in BLO, sc in each st around [9]

Rnds 8–18: sc in each st around [9]

Stuff with fiberfill. Fasten off and weave in ends.

Repeat **Rnds 1–18** for the second leg, do not fasten off after **Rnd 18**.

Rnd 19: sc 6 in second leg, do not finish rnd, this is the new starting point for the next rnd [6]

Join the two legs together by placing them next to each other (1).

Rnd 20: ch 1, sc 1 in the first leg in the inside st that is touching the second leg (2), sc 8 around first leg, sc 1 in ch, sc 9 around 2nd leg, sc 1 in the back loop of the chain st [20] (3)

Rnd 21: Sc in each st around [20]

Rnd 22: (sc 4, 2 sc in next st) repeat 4 times [24]

Rnd 23: sc in each st around [24]

Rnd 24: (sc 5, 2 sc in next st) repeat 4 times [28]

Rnd 25: change to **light pink** yarn, working in BLO, sc in each st around [28]

Rnd 26: working in BLO, (sc 5, sc2tog) repeat 4 times [24]

Rnd 27: (sc 4, sc2tog) repeat 4 times [20]

Rnd 28: sc in each st around [20]

Rnd 29: (sc 3, sc2tog) repeat 4 times [16]

Rnds 30–31: sc in each st around [16]

Rnd 32: (sc 6, sc2tog) repeat 2 times [14]

Rnd 33: change to **tan** yarn, sc in each st around [14]

Rnd 34: (sc 5, sc2tog) repeat 2 times [12]

Rnd 35: sc in each st around [12]

Rnd 36: 2 sc in each st around [24]

Rnd 37: (sc 3, 2 sc in next st) repeat 6 times [30]

Rnds 38–43: sc in each st around [30]

Place 6mm safety eyes between **Rnds 39 and 40** with 5 sts in between. Embroider a **tan** nose between **Rnds 38 and 39**, 2 sts wide. Continue stuffing with fiberfill.

Rnd 44: (sc 3, sc2tog) repeat 6 times [24]

Rnd 45: (sc 2, sc2tog) repeat 6 times [18]

Rnd 46: (sc 1, sc2tog) repeat 6 times [12]

Rnd 47: (sc2tog) repeat 6 times [6]

Fasten off and leave a long yarn tail. With yarn needle, weave the tail through FLO to close the opening. Fasten off and weave in ends.

Rnd 48: join **dark pink** yarn in FLO of **Rnd 24**, ch 1, (3 hdc in next st, sc 1) repeat 14 times [56]

Rnds 49–51: hdc in each st around [56]

Rnd 52: (ch 2, skip 1, sl st 1) repeat 14 times [42]

Fasten off and weave in ends.

Rnd 53: join **light pink** yarn in FLO of **Rnd 25**, ch 1, (3 hdc in next st, sc 1) repeat 12 times [48]

Rnds 54–55: hdc in each st around [48]

Rnd 56: (ch 2, skip 1, sl st 1) repeat 12 times [36]

Fasten off and weave in ends.

With **light pink** yarn, embroider stitches for the straps of the ballet shoes.

HAIR

Rnd 1: with **brown** yarn, sc 6 in magic loop [6]

Rnd 2: 2 sc in each st around [12]

Rnd 3: (sc 1, 2 sc in next st) repeat 6 times [18]

Rnd 4: working in BLO, (sc 2, 2 sc in next st) repeat 6 times [24]

Rnd 5: (sc 3, 2 sc in next st) repeat 6 times [30]

Rnds 6–9: sc in each st around

Continue crocheting in Rows

Row 10: sc 17, leave remaining sts unworked, turn [17]

Row 11: ch 1, sc 30, turn [30]

Row 12: ch 1, sc 30, do not turn [30]

Rnd 13: sl st in the side sts from **Rows 10 and 11**, continue to sl st in each st around [34]

Invisible fasten off (see Finishing: Invisible Fasten Off) and weave in ends.

HAIR BUN

Rnd 1: with **brown** yarn, sc 6 in magic loop [6]

Rnd 2: 2 sc in each st around [12]

Rnd 3: (sc 1, 2 sc in next st) repeat 6 times [18]

Rnds 4–5: sc in each st around [18]

Fasten off and leave a long yarn tail. Stuff the hair bun with fiberfill. With the yarn tail, sew the bun to the FLO of **Rnd 3** of the hair.

HAIR FLOWER

Rnd 1: with **dark pink** yarn, ch 3, dc in 3rd ch from hook, ch 2, sl st in same ch st, working in same ch st (ch 2 + dc 1 + ch 2 + sl st) repeat 4 times [5 petals]

Fasten off and weave in ends.
Attach to the hair bun.

ARMS (MAKE 2)

Rnd 1: with **tan** yarn, sc 6 in magic loop [6]

Rnd 2: (sc 2, 2 sc in next st) repeat 2 times [8]

Rnds 3–4: sc in each st around [8]

Rnd 5: (sc 2, sc2tog) repeat 2 times [6]

Rnds 6–14: sc in each st around [6]

Stuff lightly with fiberfill. Fasten off and leave a long yarn tail. Sew the opening of the arm closed.

With yarn needle and yarn tail sew the arms on to each side of the body between **Rnds 33 and 34**. Weave in ends.

To make the dress straps, join **light pink** yarn between **Rnds 32 and 33** near the armpit on the back side of body, ch 5, sl st near the armpit on the front side of body. Repeat a second time near the other arm. Fasten off and weave in ends.

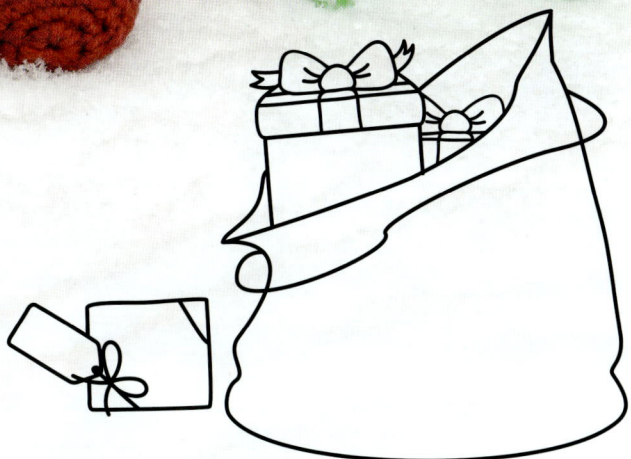

SANTA GNOME

LET'S MAKE SANTA-MENTAL MEMORIES!

Materials

- 2.75mm (C/2) crochet hook
- Paintbox Yarns Cotton DK yarn: one 50g (1¾oz) ball each of Pillar Red (**red**), Paper White (**white**), Light Caramel (**tan**), and Pure Black (**black**)
- Fiberfill stuffing
- Yarn needle
- Stitch marker

Finished Size

14cm (5½in) tall by 9cm (3½in) wide

Gauge

6 sc sts and 7 rows = 2.5cm (1in)

GNOME

Rnd 1: with **red** yarn, sc 6 in magic loop [6]

Rnd 2: sc in each st around [6]

Rnd 3: 2 sc in each st around [12]

Rnd 4: sc in each st around [12]

Rnd 5: (sc 2, 2 sc in next st) repeat 4 times [16]

Rnd 6: sc in each st around [16]

Rnd 7: (sc 3, 2 sc in next st) repeat 4 times [20]

Rnd 8: sc in each st around [20]

Rnd 9: (sc 4, 2 sc in next st) repeat 4 times [24]

Rnd 10: sc in each st around [24]

Rnd 11: (sc 5, 2 sc in next st) repeat 4 times [28]

Rnd 12: sc in each st around [28]

Rnd 13: (sc 6, 2 sc in next st) repeat 4 times [32]

Rnd 14: sc in each st around [32]

Rnd 15: (sc 7, 2 sc in next st) repeat 4 times [36]

Rnd 16: sc in each st around [36]

Rnd 17: (sc 8, 2 sc in next st) repeat 4 times [40]

Rnd 18: sc in each st around [40]

Rnd 19: working in BLO, sc in each st around [40]

Rnds 20–21: sc in each st around [40]

Rnd 22: (sc 9, 2 sc in next st) repeat 4 times [44]

Rnds 23–26: sc in each st around [44]

Rnd 27: (sc 10, 2 sc in next st) repeat 4 times [48]

Rnds 28–29: sc in each st around [48]

Rnd 30: (sc 4, sc2tog) repeat 8 times [40]

Rnds 31–33: sc in each st around [40]

Rnd 34: (sc 3, sc2tog) repeat 8 times [32]

Rnd 35: working in BLO, sc in each st around [32]

Rnd 36: (sc 2, sc2tog) repeat 8 times [24]

Rnd 37: (sc 1, sc2tog) repeat 8 times [16]

Rnd 38: (sc2tog) repeat 8 times [8]

Stuff with fiberfill. Fasten off and leave a long yarn tail. With a yarn needle weave the tail through FLO to close opening, weave in ends (see Making Up: Closing Stitches Through Front Loops).

Begin shaping by inserting needle, threaded with **red** yarn, from center bottom to center top, insert needle back down from center top to slightly off-center bottom. Insert needle from center bottom to center top. Pull to create an indentation in the bottom of the gnome (see Making Up: Shaping).

Fasten off and weave in ends.

HAT TRIM

Rnd 1: join **white** yarn in FLO of **Rnd 19**, sc in each st around [40]

Rnd 2: (skip 1, dc 5, skip 1, sl st 1) repeat 10 times [60]

BEARD

Rnd 1: with **white** yarn, sc 6 in magic loop [6]

Rnd 2: sc in each st around [6]

Rnd 3: 2 sc in each st around [12]

Rnd 4: sc 2, 2 hdc in next 2 sts, sc 4, 2 hdc in next 2 sts, sc 2 [16]

Rnd 5: sc 3, 2 hdc in next 2 sts, sc 6, 2 hdc in next 2 sts, sc 3 [20]

Rnd 6: sc 4, 2 hdc in next 2 sts, sc 8, 2 hdc in next 2 sts, sc 4 [24]

Rnd 7: sc 5, 2 hdc in next 2 sts, sc 10, 2 hdc in next 2 sts, sc 5 [28]

Rnds 8–9: sc in each st around [28]

Rnd 10: sc 5, (sc2tog) repeat 2 times, sc 10, (sc2tog) repeat 2 times, sc 5 [24]

Rnd 11: sc 4, (sc2tog) repeat 2 times, sc 8, (sc2tog) repeat 2 times, sc 4 [20]

Rnd 12: sc 3, (sc2tog) repeat 2 times, sc 6, (sc2tog) repeat 2 times, sc 3 [16]

Do not stuff with fiberfill. Fasten off and leave a long yarn tail. Sew the opening of the beard closed.

With yarn tail, sew the beard to **Rnd 20** of the gnome. Fasten off and weave in ends.

NOSE

Rnd 1: with **tan** yarn, sc 5 in magic loop [5]

Rnd 2: 2 sc in each st around [10]

Rnd 3: (sc 1, 2 sc in next st) repeat 5 times [15]

Rnd 4: working in BLO, sc in each st around [15]

Rnd 5: (sc 1, sc2tog) repeat 5 times [10]

Rnd 6: (sc2tog) repeat 5 times [5]

Stuff with fiberfill. Fasten off and leave a long yarn tail. With a yarn needle weave the tail through FLO to close opening, weave in ends (see Making Up: Closing Stitches Through Front Loops).

Attach the nose to the beard.

ARMS (MAKE 2)

Rnd 1: with **tan** yarn, sc 4 in magic loop [4]

Rnd 2: 2 sc in each st around [8]

Rnds 3–4: sc in each st around [8]

Rnd 5: change to **red** yarn, working in BLO, sc in each st around [8]

Rnds 6–9: sc in each st around [8]

Stuff lightly with fiberfill. Fasten off and leave a long yarn tail. Sew the opening of the arm closed.

Rnd 10: join **red** yarn to any FLO of **Rnd 4**, sc in each st around [8]

Fasten off and weave in ends.

Repeat **Rnds 1–10** for the second arm.

With a yarn needle and the yarn tail, sew the arms to each side of the body between **Rnds 21 and 22**. Weave in ends.

FEET (MAKE 2)

Rnd 1: with **black** yarn, sc 5 in magic loop [5]

Rnd 2: 2 sc in each st around [10]

Rnd 3: (sc 1, 2 sc in next st) repeat 5 times [15]

Rnd 4: working in BLO, sc in each st around [15]

Rnd 5: sc in each st around [15]

Rnd 6: (sc 1, sc2tog) repeat 5 times [10]

Rnd 7: (sc2tog) repeat 5 times [5]

Stuff with fiberfill. Fasten off and leave a long yarn tail. With a yarn needle weave the tail through FLO to close opening, weave in ends.

Attach the feet to the gnome between **Rnds 30 and 34**, 2.5cm (1in) apart.

CHOCOLATE REINDEER CAKE

GOOD THINGS CRUMB TO THOSE WHO BAKE

Materials

- 3.5mm (E/4) and 2.75mm (C/2) crochet hooks
- Paintbox Yarns Cotton Aran yarn: one 50g (1¾oz) ball each of Coffee Bean (**dark brown**), Light Caramel (**tan**), and Spearmint Green (**green**)
- Paintbox Yarns Cotton DK yarn: one 50g (1¾oz) ball of Coffee Bean (**dark brown**), Light Caramel (**tan**), and Pillar Red (**red**)
- 7mm safety eyes
- Scraps of **black** and **red** yarn
- Fiberfill stuffing
- Yarn needle
- Tapestry needle
- Stitch marker

Finished Size

11.5cm (4½in) tall by 7.5cm (3in) wide

Gauge

5 sc sts and 6 rows = 2.5cm (1in) using Aran yarn

CAKE

Rnd 1: with **3.5mm** hook and **dark brown Aran** yarn, sc 6 in magic loop [6]

Rnd 2: 2 sc in each st around [12]

Rnd 3: (sc 1, 2 sc in next st) repeat 6 times [18]

Rnd 4: (sc 2, 2 sc in next st) repeat 6 times [24]

Rnd 5: (sc 3, 2 sc in next st) repeat 6 times [30]

Rnd 6: (sc 4, 2 sc in next st) repeat 6 times [36]

Rnd 7: (sc 5, 2 sc in next st) repeat 6 times [42]

Rnd 8: working in BLO, sc in each st around [42]

Rnds 9–10: sc in each st around [42]

Rnd 11: change to **tan Aran** yarn, sc in each st around [42]

Rnd 12: change to **dark brown Aran** yarn, sc in each st around [42]

Rnds 13–14: sc in each st around [42]

Rnd 15: change to **tan Aran** yarn, sc in each st around [42]

Rnd 16: change to **dark brown Aran** yarn, sc in each st around [42]

Rnds 17–18: sc in each st around [42]

Place 7mm safety eyes between **Rnds 11 and 12** with 4 sts in between. Begin to stuff with fiberfill.

Rnd 19: working in BLO, (sc 5, sc2tog) repeat 6 times [36]

Rnd 20: (sc 4, sc2tog) repeat 6 times [30]

Rnd 21: (sc 3, sc2tog) repeat 6 times [24]

Rnd 22: (sc 2, sc2tog) repeat 6 times [18]

Rnd 23: (sc 1, sc2tog) repeat 6 times [12]

Rnd 24: (sc2tog) repeat 6 times [6]

Finish stuffing with fiberfill. Fasten off and leave a long yarn tail. With a yarn needle, weave the tail through FLO to close opening, weave in ends (see Making Up: Closing Stitches Through Front Loops).

Stitch the mouth and cheeks using **black** and **red** yarn (see Making Up: Stitching Facial Details).

Begin shaping by inserting needle, threaded with **dark brown Aran** yarn, from the center bottom to center top, insert needle back down from center top to slightly off-center bottom. Insert needle from center bottom to center top. Pull to create an indentation in the bottom of the cake (see Making Up: Shaping).

Fasten off and weave in ends.

FROSTING (MAKE 2)

With **3.5mm** hook and **dark brown Aran** yarn

Row 1: (ch 4, 5-dc-bl in 4th ch from hook) repeat 12 times, ch 1 [12 bobble sts]

Fasten off and weave in ends. Attach the frosting to the top edge of the cake.

Repeat **Row 1** with **green Aran** yarn for a second frosting piece. Attach the second frosting to the bottom edge of the cake.

NOSE

Rnd 1: with **2.75mm** hook and **red DK** yarn, sc 5 in magic loop [5]

Rnd 2: 2 sc in each st around [10]

Invisible fasten off (see Finishing: Invisible Fasten Off) and attach to the front of the cake in between the eyes.

BERRIES (MAKE 6)

Rnd 1: with **2.75mm** hook and **red DK** yarn, sc 4 in magic loop [4]

Rnd 2: sc in each st around [4]

Do not stuff with fiberfill. Fasten off and leave a long yarn tail. With a yarn needle, weave the tail through FLO to close the opening. Fasten off and weave in ends.

Repeat **Rnds 1–2** five more times for a total of six berries. Attach one berry in between every second bobble stitch of the green frosting.

ANTLERS (MAKE 2)

Rnd 1: with **2.75mm** hook and **tan DK** yarn, sc 6 in magic loop [6]

Rnd 2: 2 sc in each st around [12]

Rnds 3–4: sc in each st around [12]

Rnd 5: (sc 2, sc2tog) repeat 3 times [9]

Rnds 6–12: sc in each st around [9]

Stuff with fiberfill. Fasten off and leave a long yarn tail. With a yarn needle, weave the tail through FLO to close the opening. With yarn tail and needle, sew the antler to the top of the cake. Fasten off and weave in ends.

ANTLER NUBS (MAKE 2)

Rnd 1: with **2.75mm** hook and **tan DK** yarn, sc 4 in magic loop

Rnd 2: 2 sc in each st around [8]

Rnds 3–4: sc in each st around [8]

Stuff with fiberfill. Fasten off and leave a long yarn tail. With yarn tail and a needle, sew the antler nub between **Rnds 5 and 7** of the antler.

Fasten off and weave in ends.

EARS (MAKE 2)

Rnd 1: with **2.75mm** hook and **dark brown DK** yarn, sc 6 in magic loop [6]

Rnd 2: (sc 1, 2 sc in next st) repeat 3 times [9]

Rnd 3: (sc 2, 2 sc in next st) repeat 3 times [12]

Rnds 4–6: sc in each st around [12]

Rnd 7: (sc 2, sc2tog) repeat 3 times [9]

Flatten the ear, do not stuff with fiberfill. Fasten off leaving a long yarn tail. With the yarn tail and a needle, sew the ear to **Rnds 5 and 6** of the top of the cake.

Fasten off and weave in ends.

PEPPERMINT ICE CREAM

SAVORING THE MO-MINT...

Materials

- 3.5mm (E/4) and 2.75mm (C/2) crochet hooks
- Paintbox Yarns Cotton Aran yarn: one 50g (1¾oz) ball each of Candyfloss Pink (**pink**), Paper White (**white**), and Pistachio Green (**light green**)
- Paintbox Yarns Cotton DK yarn: one 50g (1¾oz) ball each of Paper White (**white**), Red Wine (**red**), and Misty Grey (**gray**)
- 8mm safety eyes
- Scraps of **red** and **black** yarn
- Fiberfill stuffing
- Yarn needle
- Stitch marker

Finished Size

12.5cm (5in) tall by 9cm (3½in) wide

Gauge

5 sc sts and 6 rows = 2.5cm (1in) using Aran yarn

ICE CREAM

Rnd 1: with **3.5mm** hook and **pink Aran** yarn, sc 6 in magic loop [6]

Rnd 2: 2 sc in each st around [12]

Rnd 3: (sc 1, 2 sc in next st) repeat 6 times [18]

Rnd 4: (sc 2, 2 sc in next st) repeat 6 times [24]

Rnd 5: (sc 3, 2 sc in next st) repeat 6 times [30]

Rnd 6: (sc 4, 2 sc in next st) repeat 6 times [36]

Rnd 7: (sc 5, 2 sc in next st) repeat 6 times [42]

Rnds 8–14: sc in each st around [42]

Place 8mm safety eyes between **Rnds 11 and 12** with 4 sts in between. Begin to stuff with fiberfill.

Rnd 15: (sc 5, sc2tog) repeat 6 times [36]

Rnd 16: (sc 4, sc2tog) repeat 6 times [30]

Rnd 17: working in BLO, (sc 3, sc2tog) repeat 6 times [24]

Rnd 18: (sc 2, sc2tog) repeat 6 times [18]

Rnd 19: (sc 1, sc2tog) repeat 6 times [12]

Rnd 20: (sc2tog) repeat 6 times [6]

Finish stuffing. Fasten off and leave a long yarn tail. With a yarn needle and the tail, weave through FLO to close opening, weave in ends.

Rnd 21: join **pink Aran** yarn in FLO of **Rnd 16**, ch 1, (2 hdc in next st, 4 hdc in next st) repeat 15 times [90]

Fasten off and weave in ends.

Add stitches for mouth and cheeks using **black** and **red** yarn (see Making Up: Stitching Facial Details).

WHIPPED CREAM

Rnd 1: with **3.5mm** hook and **white Aran** yarn, sc 6 in magic loop [6]

Rnd 2: 2 sc in each st around [12]

Rnd 3: (sc 1, 2 sc in next st) repeat 6 times [18]

Rnd 4: (sc 2, 2 sc in next st) repeat 6 times [24]

Rnd 5: (sc 1, ch 8, hdc in 2nd ch from hook, hdc in next 6 ch sts, sc in same st as ch 8, sc 1, ch 3, hdc in 2nd ch from hook, hdc in next ch st, sc in same st as ch 3, sc 2, ch 5, hdc in 2nd ch from hook, hdc in next 3 ch sts, sc in same st as ch 5, sc 2) repeat 2 times, (sc 1, ch 4, hdc in 2nd ch from hook, hdc in next 2 ch sts, sc in same st as ch 4, sc 1, ch 3, hdc in 2nd ch from hook, hdc in next ch st, sc in same st as ch 3, sc 2, ch 5, hdc in 2nd ch from hook, hdc in next 3 ch sts, sc in same st as ch 5, sc 2) repeat 2 times

Fasten off and weave in ends. Attach whipped cream to the top of the ice cream.

PEPPERMINT DISKS (MAKE 3)

Rnd 1: with **2.75mm** hook and **white DK** yarn, sc 6 in magic loop [6]

Rnd 2: 2 sc in each st around [12]

Rnd 3: (sc 1, 2 sc in next st) repeat 6 times [18]

Rnd 4: (sc 2, change to **red DK** yarn, 2 sc in next st, change to **white DK** yarn) repeat 6 times [24]

Rnd 5: working in BLO, (sc 2, change to **red DK** yarn, sc 2, change to **white DK** yarn) repeat 6 times [24]

Rnd 6: (sc 2, change to **red DK** yarn, sc 2, change to **white DK** yarn) repeat 6 times [24]

Rnd 7: working in BLO, (sc 2, change to **red DK** yarn, sc2tog, change to **white DK** yarn) repeat 6 times [18]

Stuff lightly with fiberfill.

Rnd 8: (sc 1, sc2tog) repeat 6 times [12]

Rnd 9: (sc2tog) repeat 6 times [6]

Fasten off and leave a long yarn tail. With a yarn needle weave the tail through FLO to close opening, weave in ends.

Make a total of three peppermint disks. Attach two disks to the top of the ice cream.

INSIDE OF DISH

Rnd 1: with **3.5mm** hook and **light green Aran** yarn sc 6 in magic loop [6]

Rnd 2: 2 sc in each st around [12]

Rnd 3: (sc 1, 2 sc in next st) repeat 6 times [18]

Rnd 4: (sc 2, 2 sc in next st) repeat 6 times [24]

Rnd 5: (sc 3, 2 sc in next st) repeat 6 times [30]

Rnd 6: (sc 4, 2 sc in next st) repeat 6 times [36]

Rnd 7: (sc 5, 2 sc in next st) repeat 6 times [42]

Rnd 8: (sc 6, 2 sc in next st) repeat 6 times [48]

Invisible fasten off (see Finishing: Invisible Fasten Off) and weave in ends.

DISH

Rnd 1: with **3.5mm** hook and **light green Aran** yarn, sc 6 in magic loop [6]

Rnd 2: 2 sc in each st around [12]

Rnd 3: (sc 1, 2 sc in next st) repeat 6 times [18]

Rnd 4: (sc 2, 2 sc in next st) repeat 6 times [24]

Rnd 5: (sc 3, 2 sc in next st) repeat 6 times [30]

Rnd 6: (sc 4, 2 sc in next st) repeat 6 times [36]

Rnd 7: (sc 5, 2 sc in next st) repeat 6 times [42]

Rnd 8: working in BLO, sc in each st around [42]

Rnds 9–11: sc in each st around [42]

Rnd 12: (sc 6, 2 sc in next st) repeat 6 times [48]

Rnd 13: change to **white Aran** yarn, sc in each st around [48]

Rnd 14: change to **light green Aran** yarn, sc in each st around [48]

Rnd 15: change to **white Aran** yarn sc in each st around [48]

Begin to stuff with fiberfill. Do not fasten off and cut yarn. Make the inside of the dish before moving on to **Rnd 16**.

Rnd 16: place the inside of the dish in the main dish and line up the stitches from **Rnd 15** of the main dish and **Rnd 8** of the inside of the dish. With the yarn used to make the dish, sc in each st around working in both loops of both pieces to join them together, join with sl st in first st [48]

Rnd 17: ch 1, sc in each st around, join with sl st in first st [48]

Rnd 18: sl st in each st around [48]

Invisible fasten off and weave in ends

Begin shaping (see Making Up: Shaping) by inserting a needle threaded with **light green Aran** yarn from center bottom to center top, insert needle back down from center top to slightly off-center bottom. Insert needle from center bottom to center top. Pull to create an indentation in the bottom of the dish. Fasten off and weave in ends.

SPOON

Rnd 1: with **2.75mm** hook and **gray DK** yarn, sc 6 in magic loop [6]

Rnd 2: (sc 1, 2 sc in next st) repeat 3 times [9]

Rnd 3: (sc 2, 2 sc in next st) repeat 3 times [12]

Rnd 4: (sc 3, 2 sc in next st) repeat 3 times [15]

Rnd 5: (sc 4, 2 sc in next st) repeat 3 times [18]

Rnds 6–8: sc in each st around [18]

Rnd 9: (sc 4, sc2tog) repeat 3 times [15]

Rnd 10: (sc 3, sc2tog) repeat 3 times [12]

Rnd 11: sc in each st around [12]

Rnd 12: (sc 2, sc2tog) repeat 3 times [9]

Rnd 13: (sc 1, sc2tog) repeat 3 times [6]

Rnds 14–28: sc in each st around [6]

Stuff the handle of the spoon with fiberfill. Fasten off and weave in ends.

Attach ice cream to inside of the dish.

HOLLY

HAPPY HOLLY-DAYS

Materials

- 3.5mm (E/4) crochet hook
- Paintbox Yarns Cotton Aran yarn: one 50g (1¾oz) ball each of Red Wine (**red**) and Racing Green (**dark green**)
- 7mm safety eyes
- Scraps of **black** and **pink** yarn
- Fiberfill stuffing
- Yarn needle
- Stitch marker

Finished Size

10cm (4in) tall by 14cm (5½in) wide

Gauge

5 sc sts and 6 rows = 2.5cm (1in)

BERRIES (MAKE 4)

Rnd 1: with **red** yarn, sc 6 in magic loop [6]

Rnd 2: 2 sc in each st around [12]

Rnd 3: (sc 1, 2 sc in next st) repeat 6 times [18]

Rnd 4: (sc 2, 2 sc in next st) repeat 6 times [24]

Rnd 5: (sc 3, 2 sc in next st) repeat 6 times [30]

Rnds 6–9: sc in each st around [30]

Place 7mm safety eyes between **Rnds 6 and 7** with 3 sts in between, begin to stuff with fiberfill.

Rnd 10: (sc 3, sc2tog) repeat 6 times [24]

Rnd 11: (sc 2, sc2tog) repeat 6 times [18]

Rnd 12: (sc 1, sc2tog) repeat 6 times [12]

Rnd 13: (sc2tog) repeat 6 times [6]

Finish stuffing with fiberfill. Fasten off and leave a long yarn tail. With a yarn needle weave the tail through FLO to close opening, weave in ends.

Stitch the mouth and cheeks using **black** and **pink** yarn (see Making Up: Stitching Facial Details).

Repeat **Rnds 1–13** for a total of four berries.

Attach all four berries together in a pyramid shape.

LEAVES (MAKE 3)

Rnd 1: with **dark green** yarn, ch 10, sc in 2nd ch from hook, sc 1, hdc 1, dc 1, 2 dc in next st, dc 1, hdc 1, sc 1, 3 sc in last ch st, working on the other side of the foundation ch, sc 1, hdc 1, dc 1, 2 dc in next st, dc 1, hdc 1, sc 2, sl st in skipped ch from beginning of ch 10 [22]

Rnd 2: (sl st 1, sc 1 + ch 2 + sl st in 2nd ch from hook + sc in same st as ch 2, sl st 1) repeat 7 times, sl st 1, ch 6, sl st in 2nd ch from hook and remaining 4 ch sts, sl st 1 [42]

Fasten off and weave in ends. Make a total of three holly leaves and attach them in between the berries.

Leaf chart

LOLLIPOP ORNAMENT

THIS ALL SEEMS ORNA-MENT TO BE...

Materials

- 3.5mm (E/4) and 2.75mm (C/2) crochet hooks
- Paintbox Yarns Cotton DK yarn: one 50g (1¾oz) ball each of Pillar Red (**red**), Paper White (**white**), Light Caramel (**tan**), and Lime Green (**lime green**)
- 8mm safety eyes
- Scrap of **black** yarn
- Fiberfill stuffing
- Yarn needle
- Stitch marker

Finished Size

11.5cm (4½in) tall by 6.5cm (2½in) wide

Gauge

6 sc sts and 7 rows = 2.5cm (1in)

CANDY

Rnd 1: with **2.75mm** hook and **red** yarn, hdc 11 in magic loop [11]

Rnd 2: 2 hdc in each st around [22]

Rnd 3: (2 hdc in next st, hdc 1) repeat 11 times [33]

Rnd 4: (2 hdc in next st, hdc 2) repeat 10 times, 2 hdc in next st, sc 1, sl st 1 [44]

Invisible fasten off (see Finishing: Invisible Fasten Off) and weave in ends (1).

Rnd 5: with right side facing, join white yarn in between **Rnds 1 and 2**, surface crochet by making a sl st in between each st and in between each round (2)

Fasten off and weave in ends (3).

Repeat **Rnds 1–5** for a second candy, do not fasten off **white** yarn.

Place 8mm safety eyes between **Rnds 2 and 3** with 5 sts in between.

Stitch the mouth using **black** yarn (see Making Up: Stitching Facial Details).

Rnd 6: join the two candy pieces using the **white** yarn from the second candy piece. Place the pieces together with right sides facing out and the second candy piece facing you. Working into BLO of **Rnd 4** of the second candy and FLO of **Rnd 4** of the first candy, sl st in each st around and stuff with fiberfill as you go [44] (4 and 5)

Fasten off and weave in ends.

STICK

Rnd 1: with **2.75mm** hook and **tan** yarn, sc 6 in magic loop [6]

Rnds 2–10: sc in each st around [6]

Stuff with fiberfill. Fasten off and leave a long yarn tail. Using the yarn tail, sew the stick to the lollipop below the mouth.

BOW

This bow pattern is the same as in the Christmas Bell Ornament and the Christmas Wreath pattern, see those projects for step photos.

With **3.5mm** hook and **lime green** yarn, ch 22

Row 1: sc in 2nd ch from hook, sc 2, hdc 5, sc 5, hdc 5, sc 2, 3 sc in last ch st, working on the other side of the foundation ch, sc 2, hdc 5, sc 5, hdc 5, sc 2, 2 sc in next st [44]

Fasten off and leave a long yarn tail.

BOW TAILS

With **3.5mm** hook and **lime green** yarn, ch 16

Row 1: hdc in 3rd ch from hook, hdc 13 [14]

Fasten off and weave in ends.

Join the ends of the bow by tying the two yarn tails together. Place the center of the bow tails behind the center of the bow. Wrap the yarn tails around the center of both pieces to secure them together. Tie a knot to secure. Attach the bow to the top of the lollipop.

Add a hanging loop using white yarn (see Making Up: Ornament Hanging Loop).

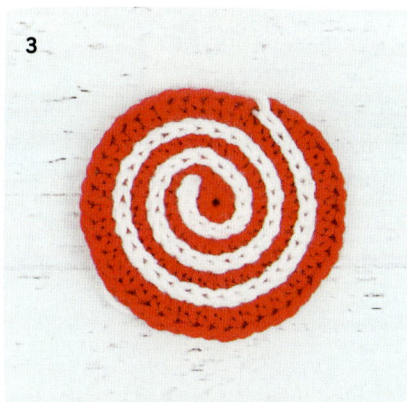

If you do not want to make this an ornament, instead of stuffing the stick with fiberfill, insert a wooden dowel the length of the stick before sewing it to the lollipop and do not add a hanging loop.

ANGEL

You've got me all aflutter!

Materials

- 2.75mm (C/2) crochet hook
- Paintbox Yarns Cotton DK yarn: one 50g (1¾oz) ball each of Champagne White (**white**), Light Caramel (**tan**), and Daffodil Yellow (**yellow**)
- Anchor Metallic Gold thread in color 303 (**metallic gold**)
- 6mm safety eyes
- Scraps of **black** and **tan** yarn
- Fiberfill stuffing
- Yarn needle
- Tapestry needle
- Stitch marker

Finished Size

12.5cm (5in) tall by 10cm (4in) wide

Gauge

6 sc sts and 7 rows = 2.5cm (1in)

BODY AND HEAD

Rnd 1: with **white** yarn, sc 6 in magic loop [6]

Rnd 2: 2 sc in each st around [12]

Rnd 3: (sc 1, 2 sc in next st) repeat 6 times [18]

Rnd 4: (sc 2, 2 sc in next st) repeat 6 times [24]

Rnd 5: (sc 3, 2 sc in next st) repeat 6 times [30]

Rnd 6: (sc 4, 2 sc in next st) repeat 6 times [36]

Rnd 7: working in BLO, sc in each st around [36]

Rnd 8: sc in each st around [36]

Rnd 9: working in BLO, sc in each st around [36]

Rnd 10: sc in each st around [36]

Rnd 11: working in BLO, (sc 4, sc2tog) repeat 6 times [30]

Rnds 12–13: sc in each st around [30]

Rnd 14: working in BLO, sc in each st around [30]

Rnd 15: sc in each st around [30]

Rnd 16: (sc 3, sc2tog) repeat 6 times [24]

Rnds 17–19: sc in each st around [24]

Rnd 20: (sc 2, sc2tog) repeat 6 times [18]

Rnds 21–22: sc in each st around [18]

Rnd 23: (sc 1, sc2tog) repeat 6 times [12]

Rnd 24: change to **tan** yarn, sc in each st around [12]

Rnd 25: 2 sc in each st around [24]

Rnd 26: (sc 3, 2 sc in next st) repeat 6 times [30]

Rnds 27–31: sc in each st around [30]

Place 6mm safety eyes between **Rnds 29 and 30** with 5 sts in between. Embroider a **tan** nose between **Rnds 28 and 29**, 2 sts wide. Embroider **black** eyelashes. Stuff with fiberfill.

Rnd 32: (sc 3, sc2tog) repeat 6 times [24]

Rnd 33: (sc 2, sc2tog) repeat 6 times [18]

Rnd 34: (sc 1, sc2tog) repeat 6 times [12]

Rnd 35: (sc2tog) repeat 6 times [6]

Fasten off and leave a long yarn tail. With a yarn needle, weave the tail through FLO to close the opening. Fasten off and weave in ends.

Rnd 36: join **metallic gold** thread in FLO of **Rnd 6**, (ch 3, sc 1) repeat 36 times [144]

Rnd 37: join **metallic gold** thread in FLO of **Rnd 8**, (ch 3, sc 1) repeat 36 times [144]

Rnd 38: join **metallic gold** thread in FLO of **Rnd 10**, (ch 3, sc 1) repeat 36 times [144]

Rnd 39: join **metallic gold** thread in FLO of **Rnd 13**, (ch 3, sc 1) repeat 30 times [120]

Begin shaping by inserting needle from center bottom to center top, insert needle back down from center top to slightly off-center bottom. Insert needle from center bottom to center top. Pull to create an indentation in the bottom of the angel (see Making Up: Shaping). Fasten off and weave in ends.

ARMS (MAKE 2)

Rnd 1: with **tan** yarn, sc 6 in magic loop [6]

Rnd 2: (sc 1, 2 sc in next st) repeat 3 times [9]

Rnds 3–4: sc in each st around [9]

Rnd 5: change to **white** yarn, working in BLO, sc in each st around [9]

Rnds 6–9: sc in each st around [9]

Stuff lightly with fiberfill. Fasten off and leave a long yarn tail. Sew the opening of the arm closed.

Rnd 10: join **metallic gold** thread in FLO of **Rnd 4**, sc in each st around [9]

Fasten off and weave in ends.

Repeat **Rnds 1–10** for the second arm.

With yarn needle and the yarn tail, sew the arms to each side of the body between **Rnds 23 and 24**. Weave in ends.

HAIR

Rnd 1: with **yellow** yarn, sc 6 in magic loop [6]

Rnd 2: 2 sc in each st around [12]

Rnd 3: (sc 1, 2 sc in next st) repeat 6 times [18]

Rnd 4: working in BLO, (sc 2, 2 sc in next st) repeat 6 times [24]

Rnd 5: (sc 3, 2 sc in next st) repeat 6 times [30]

Rnds 6–7: sc in each st around

Continue crocheting in Rows

Row 8: sc 17, leave remaining sts unworked, turn [17]

Row 9: ch 1, sc 30, turn [30]

Row 10: ch 1, sc 30, do not turn [30]

Rnd 11: sl st in the side sts from **Rows 8 and 9**, continue to sl st in each st around [34]

Invisible fasten off (see Finishing: Invisible Fasten Off) and weave in ends.

HAIR BUN

Rnd 1: with **yellow** yarn, sc 6 in magic loop [6]

Rnd 2: 2 sc in each st around [12]

Rnd 3: (sc 1, 2 sc in next st) repeat 6 times [18]

Rnds 4–5: sc in each st around [18]

Fasten off and leave a long yarn tail. Stuff the bun with fiberfill. With the yarn tail, sew the bun to the FLO of **Rnd 3** of the hair.

HAIR RIBBON

Rnd 1: with **metallic gold** thread, ch 19, sl st in first ch st to make a circle, sc in each st around [18]

Fasten off and weave in ends. Place the ribbon around the base of the bun.

WINGS (MAKE 2)

With **white** yarn, ch 7

Row 1: sc in 2nd ch from hook, sc 5, turn [6]

Row 2: ch 1, sc 2, 2 sc in next st, sc 2, leave last st unworked, turn [6]

Row 3: ch 3, sc in 2nd ch from hook, sc in next ch, sc 3, 2 sc in next st, sc 2, turn [9]

Row 4: ch 1, sc 3, 2 sc in next st, sc 4, skip last st, turn [9]

Row 5: ch 3, sc in 2nd ch from hook, sc in next ch, sc 5, 2 sc in next st, sc 3, turn [12]

Row 6: ch 1, sc 2, 2 sc in next st, sc 8, skip last st, turn [12]

Row 7: ch 3, sc in 2nd ch from hook, sc in next ch, sc 8, 2 sc in next st, sc 3, turn [15]

Fasten off and leave a long yarn tail.

Repeat **Rows 1–7** for the second wing.

Using the yarn tails, sew the wings to the angel's back.

CHRISTMAS WREATH

ALL YOU NEEDLE IS LOVE...

Materials

- 3.5mm (E/4) crochet hook
- Paintbox Yarns Cotton Aran yarn: one 50g (1¾oz) ball each of Spearmint Green (**green**), Pillar Red (**red**), and Racing Green (**dark green**)
- 8mm safety eyes
- Scraps of **black** and **red** yarn
- Fiberfill stuffing
- Yarn needle
- Stitch marker

Finished Size

10cm (4in) tall by 10cm (4in) wide

Gauge

5 sc sts and 6 rows = 2.5cm (1in)

WREATH

With **green** yarn, ch 30

Rnd 1: join with sl st in first ch to form a circle, sc in each st around [30]

Rnd 2: (sc 2, 2 sc in next st) repeat 10 times [40]

Rnd 3: (sc 3, 2 sc in next st) repeat 10 times [50]

Rnds 4–11: sc in each st around [50]

Rnd 12: (sc 3, sc2tog) repeat 10 times [40]

Rnd 13: (sc 2, sc2tog) repeat 10 times [30]

Rnd 14: sc in each st around [30]

Rnd 15: working in BLO, sc in each st around [30]

Rnds 16–17: sc in each st around [30]

Place 8mm safety eyes between **Rnds 12 and 13** with 4 sts in between.

Fasten off and leave a long yarn tail. Using a yarn needle and the tail, sew **Rnd 17** to **Rnd 1** and stuff with fiberfill as you go.

Stitch the mouth and cheeks using **black** and **red** yarn (see Making Up: Stitching Facial Details).

HOLLY LEAVES (MAKE 2)

With **dark green** yarn, ch 10

Rnd 1: sc in 2nd ch from hook, sc 1, hdc 1, dc 1, 2 dc in next st, dc 1, hdc 1, sc 1, 3 sc in last ch st, working on the other side of the foundation ch, sc 1, hdc 1, dc 1, 2 dc in next st, dc 1, hdc 1, sc 2, sl st in skipped ch from beginning of ch 10 [22]

Rnd 2: (sl st 1, sc 1 + ch 2 + sl st in 2nd ch from hook + sc in same st as ch 2, sl st 1) repeat 7 times [35]

Fasten off and weave in ends. Make a total of two holly leaves and attach them to the top-front of the wreath.

BOW

With **red** yarn, ch 22

Row 1: sc in 2nd ch from hook, sc 2, hdc 5, sc 5, hdc 5, sc 2, 3 sc in last ch st, working on the other side of the foundation ch, sc 2, hdc 5, sc 5, hdc 5, sc 2, 2 sc in next st [44]

Fasten off and leave a long yarn tail (1).

BOW TAILS

With **red** yarn, ch 16

Row 1: hdc in 3rd ch from hook, hdc 13 [14]

Fasten off and weave in ends.

Join the ends of the bow by tying the two yarn tails together. Place the center of the bow tails behind the center of the bow. Wrap the yarn tails around the center of both pieces to attach them (2). Tie a knot to secure.

Attach the bow to the top of the wreath.

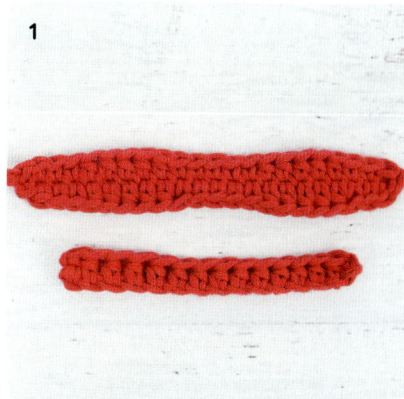

Leaf chart

SANTA CLAUS

CHRISTMAS HAS ME FEELING
EXTRA SANTA-MENTAL

BODY AND HEAD

Rnd 1: with **black** yarn, sc 6 in magic loop [6]

Rnd 2: 2 sc in each st around [12]

Rnd 3: (sc 1, 2 sc in next st) repeat 6 times [18]

Rnd 4: sc in each st around [18]

Rnd 5: sc 2, (sc2tog) repeat 4 times, sc 8 [14]

Rnd 6: sc 2, (sc2tog) repeat 2 times, sc 8 [12]

Rnd 7: sc 8, do not finish rnd, new starting point should be center-back of leg [8]

Rnd 8: change to **red** yarn, working in BLO, sc in each st around [12]

Rnds 9–12: sc in each st around [12]

Invisible fasten off (see Finishing: Invisible Fasten Off) and weave in ends. Stuff with fiberfill.

Rnd 13: join **black** yarn in FLO of **Rnd 7**, sl st in each st around [12]

Fasten off and weave in ends.

Repeat **Rnds 1–13** for a second leg, do not fasten off after **Rnd 12**.

Continue working in second leg to join the two legs together.

Begin the next rnd in the next leg after making the ch 3 (1).

Rnd 14: ch 3, sc 12, sc 3 along the chain (2), sc 12 around next leg (3), 2 sc in next ch st, sc 1, 2 sc in next ch st into the back loops of the chain sts (4) [32]

Rnd 15: sc 13, do not finish rnd, new starting point should be center-back of legs [13]

Rnd 16: working in BLO, sc in each st around [32]

Rnds 17–18: sc in each st around [32]

Rnd 19: change to **black** yarn, sc in each st around [32]

Rnd 20: sc in each st around [32]

Rnd 21: change to **red** yarn, sc in each st around [32]

Rnd 22: sc 8, sc2tog, sc 14, sc2tog, sc 6 [30]

Rnd 23: (sc 3, sc2tog) repeat 6 times [24]

Rnd 24: sc in each st around [24]

Rnd 25: (sc 2, sc2tog) repeat 6 times [18]

Rnd 26: sc in each st around [18]

Rnd 27: (sc 1, sc2tog) repeat 6 times [12]

Rnd 28: change to **tan** yarn, sc in each st around [12]

Rnd 29: 2 sc in each st around [24]

Rnd 30: (sc 3, 2 sc in next st) repeat 6 times [30]

Rnds 31–36: sc in each st around [30]

Place 6mm safety eyes between **Rnds 33 and 34** with 6 sts in between. Embroider a pink nose between **Rnds 32 and 33**, 2 sts wide. Continue stuffing with fiberfill.

How many names does Santa Claus have? Some well-known nicknames include: Santa, St Nick, Father Christmas, The Big Man in Red, St Nicholas, Kris Kringle, and even Captain Christmas.

Rnd 37: (sc 3, sc2tog) repeat 6 times [24]

Rnd 38: (sc 2, sc2tog) repeat 6 times [18]

Rnd 39: (sc 1, sc2tog) repeat 6 times [12]

Rnd 40: (sc2tog) repeat 6 times [6]

Fasten off and leave a long yarn tail. With a yarn needle, weave the tail through FLO to close the opening. Weave in ends.

Rnd 41: join **white novelty** yarn in FLO of **Rnd 15**, sc 32 [32]

Fasten off and weave in ends.

Embroider a buckle on the black belt with **metallic gold** thread, 3 sts wide and 1 st tall.

ARMS (MAKE 2)

Rnd 1: with **tan** yarn, sc 6 in magic loop [6]

Rnd 2: (sc 1, 2 sc in next st) repeat 3 times [9]

Rnds 3–4: sc in each st around [9]

Rnd 5: change to **red** yarn, working in BLO, sc in each st around [9]

Rnds 6–10: sc in each st around [9]

Stuff lightly with fiberfill. Fasten off and leave a long yarn tail. Sew the opening of the arm closed.

Rnd 11: join **white novelty yarn** in FLO of **Rnd 4**, sc in each st around [9]

Fasten off and weave in ends.

Repeat **Rnds 1–11** for the second arm.

With a yarn needle and the yarn tail, sew the arms to each side of the body between **Rnds 26 and 27**. Weave in ends.

BEARD

With **white novelty** yarn, begin with a 23cm (9in) yarn tail and ch 7

Row 1: sc 1 in 2nd ch from hook, sc 5, turn [6]

Row 2: ch 1, sc2tog, sc 2, sc2tog, turn [4]

Row 3: ch 1, sc in each st across, turn [4]

Row 3: ch 1, (sc2tog) repeat 2 times, turn [2]

Row 4: ch 1, sc2tog [1]

Fasten off, leaving a long yarn tail. With the yarn tail, sew the beard under the eyes and nose.

HAT

Rnd 1: with **red** yarn, sc 6 in magic loop [6]

Rnd 2: sc in each st around [6]

Rnd 3: (sc 1, 2 sc in next st) repeat 3 times [9]

Rnd 4: sc in each st around [9]

Rnd 5: (sc 2, 2 sc in next st) repeat 3 times [12]

Rnds 6–7: sc in each st around [12]

Rnd 8: (sc 3, 2 sc in next st) repeat 3 times [15]

Rnds 9–10: sc in each st around [15]

Rnd 11: (sc 4, 2 sc in next st) repeat 3 times [18]

Rnds 12–13: sc in each st around [18]

Rnd 14: (sc 5, 2 sc in next st) repeat 3 times [21]

Rnds 15–16: sc in each st around [21]

Rnd 17: (sc 6, 2 sc in next st) repeat 3 times [24]

Rnds 18–19: sc in each st around [24]

Rnd 20: (sc 7, 2 sc in next st) repeat 3 times [27]

Rnd 21: sc in each st around [27]

Rnd 22: (sc 8, 2 sc in next st) repeat 3 times [30]

Rnd 23: sc in each st around [30]

Rnd 24: (sc 9, 2 sc in next st) repeat 3 times [33]

Rnd 25: sc in each st around [33]

Rnd 26: change to **white novelty** yarn, working in FLO, sc in each st around [33]

Invisible fasten off and weave in ends.

Fold white brim up.

POM-POM

Rnd 1: with **white novelty** yarn, sc 5 in magic loop [5]

Rnd 2: 2 sc in each st around [10]

Rnd 3: (sc2tog) repeat 5 times [5]

Fasten off and leave a long yarn tail. With a yarn needle, weave the tail through FLO to close the opening. Fasten off and weave in ends. Attach the pom-pom to **Rnd 1** of the hat and bend the top of the hat down and secure at **Rnd 14**.

MINI MITTENS

Materials

- 2.75mm (C/2) crochet hook
- Paintbox Yarns Cotton DK yarn: one 50g (1¾oz) ball each of Pillar Red (**red**) and Paper White (**white**)
- 6mm safety eyes
- Scraps of **black** and **pink** yarn
- Fiberfill stuffing
- Yarn needle
- Stitch marker

Finished Size

6.5cm (2½in) tall by 5cm (2in) wide (one mitten)

Gauge

6 sc sts and 7 rows = 2.5cm (1in)

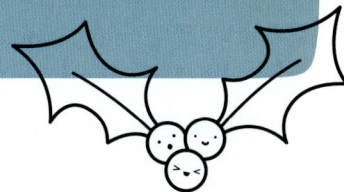

> **I'M SO SMITTEN WITH YOU!**

THUMBS (MAKE 2)

Rnd 1: with **red** yarn, sc 6 in magic loop [6]

Rnd 2: (sc 2, 2 sc in next st) repeat 2 times [8]

Rnds 3–4: sc in each st around [8]

Fasten off and leave a long yarn tail.

MITTENS (MAKE 2)

Rnd 1: with **red** yarn, sc 6 in magic loop [6]

Rnd 2: 2 sc in each st around [12]

Rnd 3: (sc 1, 2 sc in next st) repeat 6 times [18]

Rnds 4–8: sc in each st around [18]

Now you will be joining the thumb to the mitten.

Rnd 9: continue working on the mitten, sc 1, begin working in the first st of **Rnd 4** of the thumb, sc 3, sc2tog, sc 2, skip last st of thumb, working on the sts of the mitten, skip 1, sc 8, sc2tog, sc 6 [22]

Rnd 10: sc 3, sc2tog, sc 9, sc2tog, sc 6 [20]

Place 6mm safety eyes between **Rnds 7 and 8** with 3 sts in between. Begin to stuff with fiberfill.

With the yarn tail from the thumb, sew the unworked sts from **Rnd 4** of the thumb and **Rnd 8** of the hand.

Rnd 11: sc 2, sc2tog, sc 8, sc2tog, sc 6 [18]

Rnd 12: sc 2, sc2tog, sc 7, sc2tog, sc 5 [16]

Rnd 13: sc 2, sc2tog, sc 6, sc2tog, sc 4 [14]

Rnd 14: join **white** yarn, hdc in each st around [14]

Rnd 15: (hdc 1, fphdc) repeat 7 times [14]

Rnd 16: sl st in each st around [14]

Invisible fasten off (see Finishing: Invisible Fasten Off), stuff lightly with fiberfill. With yarn tail, sew opening closed. Weave in ends.

Stitch the mouth and cheeks using **black** and **pink** yarn (see Making Up: Stitching Facial Details).

Repeat **Rnds 1–16** for a second mitten.

Note: When making the second mitten, at the end of **Rnd 13**, crochet an additional sc 5, so the color join will only be visible from the back.

MITTEN MINDER CORD

Join the **white** yarn on the upper side of the cuff of the first mitten just above the thumb, ch 20, sl st on the upper side of the cuff of the second mitten just above the thumb, sl st in the back bump or bar of each ch st (see Special Stitches).

Fasten off and weave in ends.

CHRISTMAS BELL ORNAMENT

IT'S IMPOSSI-BELL NOT TO FEEL FESTIVE RIGHT NOW

Materials

- 3.5mm (E/4) crochet hook
- Paintbox Yarns Cotton Aran yarn: one 50g (1¾oz) ball each of Glorious Gold (**gold**) and Red Wine (**red**)
- 7mm safety eyes
- Scraps of **black** and **red** yarn
- Fiberfill stuffing
- Yarn needle
- Stitch marker

Finished Size

6.5cm (2½in) tall by 6.5cm (2½in) wide

Gauge

5 sc sts and 6 rows = 2.5cm (1in)

BELL

Rnd 1: with **gold** yarn, sc 6 in magic loop [6]

Rnd 2: 2 sc in each st around [12]

Rnd 3: (sc 1, 2 sc in next st) repeat 6 times [18]

Rnd 4: (sc 2, 2 sc in next st) repeat 6 times [24]

Rnds 5–12: sc in each st around [24]

Place 7mm safety eyes between **Rnds 8 and 9** with 3 sts in between.

Rnd 13: (sc 3, 2 sc in next st) repeat 6 times [30]

Rnd 14: (sc 4, 2 sc in next st) repeat 6 times [36]

Rnd 15: working under the sts from **Rnd 14** and into **Rnd 13**, (sc 4, 2 sc in next st) repeat 6 times [36]

Rnd 16: sl st in each st around [36]

Invisible fasten off and weave in ends (see Finishing: Invisible Fasten Off).

Stitch the mouth and cheeks using **black** and **red** yarn (see Making Up: Stitching Facial Details).

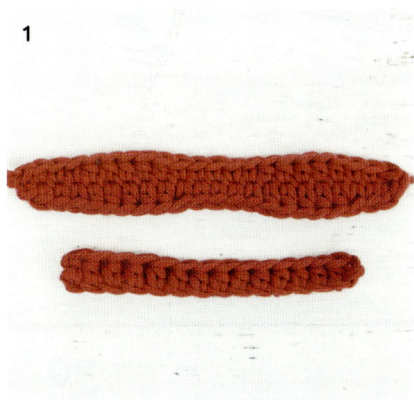

CLAPPER

Rnd 1: with **gold** yarn, sc 6 in magic loop [6]

Rnd 2: 2 sc in each st around [12]

Rnds 3−4: sc in each st around [12]

Rnd 5: (sc2tog) repeat 6 times [6]

Stuff with fiberfill. Fasten off and leave a long yarn tail. With a yarn needle weave the tail through FLO to close opening.

With the same yarn tail, sew the clapper to the inside top of the bell, leaving 7.5cm (3in) of yarn between the clapper and the top of the bell.

With the same yarn tail make a 4cm (1½in) loop with the yarn so the bell can be hung as an ornament (see Making Up: Ornament Hanging Loop).

BOW

With **red** yarn, ch 22

Row 1: sc in 2nd ch from hook, sc 2, hdc 5, sc 5, hdc 5, sc 2, 3 sc in last ch st, working on the other side of the foundation ch, sc 2, hdc 5, sc 5, hdc 5, sc 2, 2 sc in next st [44]

Fasten off and leave a long yarn tail (1).

BOW TAILS

With **red** yarn, ch 16

Row 1: ch 16, hdc in 3rd ch from hook, hdc 13 [14]

Fasten off and weave in ends.

Join the ends of the bow by tying the two yarn tails together. Place the center of the bow tails behind the center of the bow. Wrap the yarn tails around the center of both pieces to attach them (2). Tie a knot to secure.

Attach the bow to the top of the bell (3).

GiFT BOX

DON'T GiFT UP!

Materials

- 3.5mm (E/4) and 2.75mm (C/2) crochet hooks
- Paintbox Yarns Cotton Aran yarn: one 50g (1¾oz) ball of Pillar Red (**red**)
- Paintbox Yarns Cotton DK yarn: one 50g (1¾oz) ball of Grass Green (**green**)
- 8mm safety eyes
- Scraps of **pink** and **black** yarn
- Cardboard
- 26-gauge floral wire
- Fiberfill stuffing
- Yarn needle
- Stitch marker

Finished Size

9cm (3½in) tall by 7.5cm (3in) wide

Gauge

5 sc sts and 6 rows = 2.5cm (1in) using Aran yarn

BOX

Rnd 1: with **3.5mm** hook and **red Aran** yarn, sc 6 in magic loop [6]

Rnd 2: 2 sc in each st around [12]

Rnd 3: sc 1, (3 sc in next st, sc 2) repeat 3 times, 3 sc in next st, sc 1 [20]

Rnd 4: sc 2, (3 sc in next st, sc 4) repeat 3 times, 3 sc in next st, sc 2 [28]

Rnd 5: sc 3, (3 sc in next st, sc 6) repeat 3 times, 3 sc in next st, sc 3 [36]

Rnd 6: sc 4, (3 sc in next st, sc 8) repeat 3 times, 3 sc in next st, sc 4 [44]

Rnd 7: working in BLO, sc in each st around [44]

Rnds 8–18: sc in each st around [44]

Fasten off and leave a 45.5cm (18in) yarn tail for sewing the top piece onto the box.

Place 8mm safety eyes between **Rnds 12 and 13** with 5 sts in between.

TOP

Rnd 1: with **3.5mm** hook and **red Aran** yarn, sc 6 in magic loop [6]

Rnd 2: 2 sc in each st around [12]

Rnd 3: sc 1, (3 sc in next st, sc 2) repeat 3 times, 3 sc in next st, sc 1 [20]

Rnd 4: sc 2, (3 sc in next st, sc 4) repeat 3 times, 3 sc in next st, sc 2 [28]

Rnd 5: sc 3, (3 sc in next st, sc 6) repeat 3 times, 3 sc in next st, sc 3 [36]

Rnd 6: sc 4, (3 sc in next st, sc 8) repeat 3 times, 3 sc in next st, sc 4 [44]

Invisible fasten off (see Finishing: Invisible Fasten Off) and weave in ends.

Trace the top piece, twice, onto cardboard and cut out.

Place a cardboard piece in the bottom of the box. Fill the box with fiberfill (1). Place the second cardboard piece on top. With a yarn needle and yarn tail, work in BLO of both pieces to sew the top piece onto the box (2).

Stitch the mouth and cheeks using **black** and **pink** yarn (see Making Up: Stitching Facial Details).

LID

Rnd 1: with **3.5mm** hook and **red Aran** yarn, sc 6 in magic loop [6]

Rnd 2: 2 sc in each st around [12]

Rnd 3: sc 1, (3 sc in next st, sc 2) repeat 3 times, 3 sc in next st, sc 1 [20]

Rnd 4: sc 2, (3 sc in next st, sc 4) repeat 3 times, 3 sc in next st, sc 2 [28]

Rnd 5: sc 3, (3 sc in next st, sc 6) repeat 3 times, 3 sc in next st, sc 3 [36]

Rnd 6: sc 4, (3 sc in next st, sc 8) repeat 3 times, 3 sc in next st, sc 4 [44]

Rnd 7: sc 5, (3 sc in next st, sc 10) repeat 3 times, 3 sc in next st, sc 5 [52]

Rnd 8: working in BLO, sc in each st around [52]

Rnds 9–10: sc in each st around [52]

Rnd 11: sl st in each st around [52]

Invisible fasten off and weave in ends (3).

RIBBON

With **2.75mm** hook and **green DK** yarn, start with a 30cm (12in) yarn tail and ch 4

Row 1: sc in 2nd ch from hook, sc 2, turn [3]

Rows 2–35: ch 1, sc 3, turn [3]

Fasten off and leave a 30cm (12in) yarn tail (4).

With a yarn needle and the yarn tail, sew each end of the ribbon to the front-top and back-top of the box (5). Place the lid on the box with the ribbon wrapping around the top of the lid (6).

BOW

With **2.75mm** hook and **green DK** yarn, ch 4

Row 1: sc in 2nd ch from hook, sc 2, turn [3]

Rows 2–80: ch 1, sc 3, turn [3]

Fasten off and weave in ends.

Shape into a bow by taking one end of the crochet ribbon and forming a large loop. Make a second large loop opposite the first loop and make a small loop in between the two large loops. Secure them in place with a U-shaped piece of floral wire by passing one end of the wire through the center loop and twisting both ends together to secure. Attach the bow to the top of the gift box (4 and 7).

WINTER PENGUIN

YOU'RE BRRR-illiANT

Materials

- 3.5mm (E/4) and 2.75mm (C/2) crochet hooks
- Paintbox Yarns Cotton Aran yarn: one 50g (1¾oz) ball each of Vanilla Cream (**white**), Granite Grey (**gray**), and Melon Sorbet (**yellow**)
- Paintbox Yarns Cotton DK yarn: one 50g (1¾oz) ball of Duck Egg Blue (**blue**)
- 8mm safety eyes
- T-pins
- Fiberfill stuffing
- Yarn needle
- Stitch marker

Finished Size

13.5cm (5¼in) tall by 10cm (4in) wide (without hat)

Gauge

5 sc sts and 6 rows = 2.5cm (1in) using Aran yarn

BODY AND HEAD

Rnd 1: with **3.5mm** hook and **gray Aran** yarn, sc 6 in magic loop [6]

Rnd 2: 2 sc in each st around [12]

Rnd 3: (sc 1, 2 sc in next st) repeat 6 times [18]

Rnd 4: (sc 2, 2 sc in next st) repeat 6 times [24]

Rnd 5: (sc 3, 2 sc in next st) repeat 6 times [30]

Rnd 6: (sc 4, 2 sc in next st) repeat 6 times [36]

Rnds 7–10: sc in each st around [36]

Rnd 11: (sc 10, sc2tog) repeat 3 times [33]

Rnd 12: sc in each st around [33]

Rnd 13: (sc 9, sc2tog) repeat 3 times [30]

Rnd 14: sc in each st around [30]

Rnd 15: (sc 8, sc2tog) repeat 3 times [27]

Rnd 16: (sc 7, sc2tog) repeat 3 times [24]

Rnd 17: (sc 6, sc2tog) repeat 3 times [21]

Rnd 18: (sc 5, sc2tog) repeat 3 times [18]

Rnd 19: (sc 2, sc2tog) repeat 6 times [12]

Rnd 20: change to **white Aran** yarn,
2 sc in each st around [24]

Rnd 21: (sc 3, 2 sc in next st) repeat 6 times [30]

Rn 22: (sc 4, 2 sc in next st) repeat 6 times [36]

Rnds 23–28: sc in each st around [36]

Place 8mm safety eyes between **Rnds 22 and 23** with 6 sts in between. Stuff with fiberfill.

Rnd 29: (sc 4, sc2tog) repeat 6 times [30]

Rnd 30: (sc 3, sc2tog) repeat 6 times [24]

Rnd 31: (sc 2, sc2tog) repeat 6 times [18]

Rnd 32: (sc 1, sc2tog) repeat 6 times [12]

Rnd 33: (sc2tog) repeat 6 times [6]

Fasten off and leave a long yarn tail. With a yarn needle, weave the tail through FLO to close the opening. Fasten off and weave in ends.

TOP OF HEAD

Rnd 1: with **3.5mm** hook and **gray Aran** yarn, sc 6 in magic loop [6]

Rnd 2: 2 sc in each st around [12]

Rnd 3: (sc 1, 2 sc in next st) repeat 6 times [18]

Rnd 4: (sc 2, 2 sc in next st) repeat 6 times [24]

Rnd 5: (sc 3, 2 sc in next st) repeat 6 times [30]

Rnd 6: (sc 4, 2 sc in next st) repeat 6 times [36]

Rnds 7–12: sc in each st around [36]

Count forward 16 sts and place a stitch marker.

Invisible fasten off (see Finishing: Invisible Fasten Off) and weave in ends. Join **gray Aran** yarn at stitch marker.

Row 13: ch 1, sc 5, turn [5]

Row 14: ch 1, sc 5, turn [5]

Row 15: ch 1, sc 3, sc2tog, turn [4]

Row 16: ch 1, sc 2, sc2tog, turn [3]

Row 17: ch 1, sc 1, sc2tog [2]

Fasten off and weave in ends. Attach to the top of the head (1 and 3).

BEAK

Rnd 1: with **3.5mm** hook and **yellow Aran** yarn, sc 6 in magic loop [6]

Rnd 2: sc in each st around [6]

Fasten off and leave a long yarn tail. With a yarn needle and the yarn tail, attach the beak in between the eyes (1).

WINGS (MAKE 2)

Rnd 1: with **3.5mm** hook and **gray Aran** yarn, sc 6 in magic loop [6]

Rnd 2: (sc 1, 2 sc in next st) repeat 3 times [9]

Rnd 3: sc in each st around [9]

Rnd 4: (sc 2, 2 sc in next st) repeat 3 times [12]

Rnd 5: sc in each st around [12]

Rnd 6: (sc 3, 2 sc in next st) repeat 3 times [15]

Rnd 7: sc in each st around [15]

Rnd 8: fold wing in half, working through stitches on both sides, sc 7 to close opening [7]

Fasten off and leave a long yarn tail. With a yarn needle and the yarn tail, attach the wings to the body (1, 2, and 3).

FEET (MAKE 2)

Rnd 1: with **3.5mm** hook and **yellow Aran** yarn, sc 6 in magic loop [6]

Rnd 2: (sc 1, 2 sc in next st) repeat 3 times [9]

Rnds 3–4: sc in each st around [9]

Fasten off and leave a long yarn tail. With a yarn needle and the yarn tail, attach the feet to the body (4 and 5).

TAIL

Rnd 1: with **3.5mm** hook and **gray Aran** yarn, sc 6 in magic loop [6]

Rnd 2: (sc 1, 2 sc in next st) repeat 3 times [9]

Fasten off and leave a long yarn tail. With a yarn needle and the yarn tail, attach the tail to the body (4 and 5).

SCARF

With **2.75mm** hook and **blue DK** yarn, ch5

Row 1: sc in 2nd ch from hook, sc 3, turn [4]

Rows 2–60: ch 1, working in BLO, sc in each st across, turn [4]

Fasten off and weave in ends. With small pieces of **blue DK** yarn, tie four tassels to each end of the scarf. Trim the ends so they are all even in length.

HAT

Rnd 1: with **2.75mm** hook and **blue DK** yarn, sc 6 in magic loop [6]

Rnd 2: 2 sc in each st around [12]

Rnd 3: (sc 1, 2 sc in next st) repeat 6 times [18]

Rnd 4: (sc 2, 2 sc in next st) repeat 6 times [24]

Rnd 5: (sc 3, 2 sc in next st) repeat 6 times [30]

Rnd 6: (sc 4, 2 sc in next st) repeat 6 times [36]

Rnd 7: (sc 5, 2 sc in next st) repeat 6 times [42]

Rnd 8: (sc 6, 2 sc in next st) repeat 6 times [48]

Rnds 9–14: sc in each st around [48]

Rnds 10–13: working in BLO, sc in each st around [48]

Invisible fasten off and weave in ends. Make a 2.5cm (1in) pom-pom and attach it to the top of the hat.

TECHNIQUES

USEFUL INFORMATION

Key to Pattern Charts

▷	Starting Point
◉	Magic Loop
⊖	Chain
⬭	Slip Stitch
✕	Single Crochet
T	Half Double Crochet
†	Double Crochet
‡	Treble Crochet
⌢	Front Loop
⌣	Back Loop
✕✕	Single Crochet Increase

Terminology

The patterns in this book are written using US crochet terms.

Conversion Chart (US to UK)

- Single Crochet (sc) = Double Crochet (dc)
- Double Crochet (dc) = Treble Crochet (tr)
- Half Double Crochet (hdc) = Half Treble Crochet (htr)
- Treble Crochet (tr) = Double Treble Crochet (dtr)

Pattern Abbreviations

- 5-dc-bl = 5 double crochet bobble
- 3-dc-bl = 3 double crochet bobble
- BLO = back loops only
- ch = chain stitch
- dc = double crochet stitch
- dc2tog = double crochet decrease
- FLO = front loops only
- fphdc = front post half double crochet
- hdc = half double crochet
- hdc2tog = half double crochet decrease
- rnd = round
- sc = single crochet stitch
- sc2tog = single crochet decrease
- sl st = slip stitch
- st(s) = stitch(es)
- tr = treble crochet stitch

Skill Levels

Beginner

Easy

Intermediate

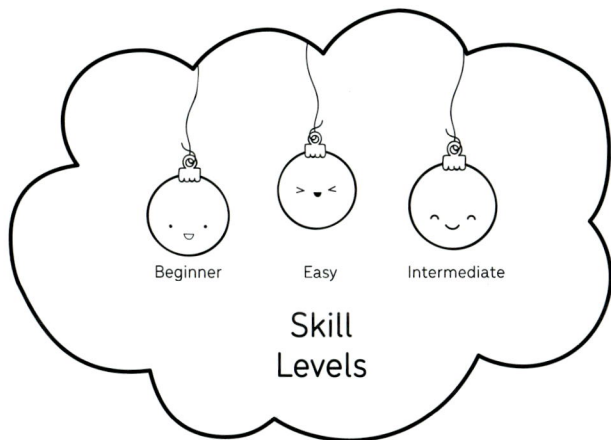

How to Read Patterns

- Abbreviations are used throughout the book, please see "Pattern Abbreviations" to see how stitches are described.

- Almost all patterns are worked in a continuous spiral; you only need to join a round if the pattern specifically instructs you to.

- If something is crocheted in rows it will begin with "Row" instead of "Rnd".

- Repetitions throughout the round are placed in parentheses, and the number of times this part is repeated is added after the parentheses. For example, **(sc 2, 2 sc in next st) 6 times**. This means to crochet 1 single crochet stitch in each of the first 2 stitches, then make 2 single crochet stitches (or a single crochet increase) in the third stitch, next the sequence of 1 single crochet in the next 2 stitches and 2 single crochet stitches in the next stitch is repeated another five times.

- A sequence of stitches worked in the same stitch is joined with a +. For example, **(sl st + ch 2 + dc 1 + ch 2 + sl st) 4 times**. This means crochet a slip stitch, chain 2, 1 double crochet, chain 2, and a slip stitch all in the next stitch and then repeat the sequence another three times.

- At the end of each line you will find the total number of stitches you should have in square brackets, for example, **[24]** means you should have 24 total stitches in that round or row once complete.

Modifying the Design

The easiest way to make your amigurumi unique is by selecting a different yarn weight to the one the pattern calls for.

For example, if you wish to make a giant Orange cushion you could use a bulky weight yarn and the amigurumi will be larger, while maintaining the same proportions. Or, if you wish to make a tiny Candy Cane keychain, you could select a fingering weight yarn and a smaller hook size. The wonderful thing about amigurumi is that when the yarn weight and corresponding hook size is changed the proportions still remain the same!

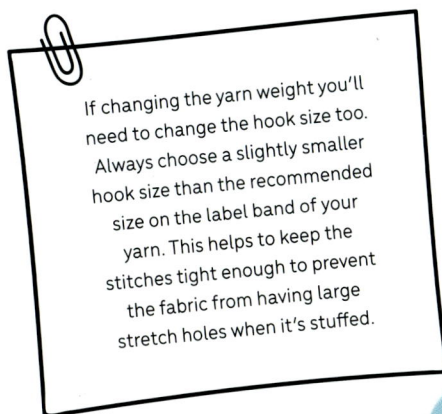

If changing the yarn weight you'll need to change the hook size too. Always choose a slightly smaller hook size than the recommended size on the label band of your yarn. This helps to keep the stitches tight enough to prevent the fabric from having large stretch holes when it's stuffed.

BASIC STITCHES

Magic Loop

With the tail end of the yarn hanging down, make a loop and hold it securely between two fingers (1).

Insert the hook into the loop and pull the working yarn through (2), make a chain stitch to secure, and begin making stitches inside the loop (3). When you've finished, pull the tail to tighten the loop.

Slip Knot

Make a loop with the tail end of the yarn hanging down (4). Insert the hook or your fingers into the loop and pull the working yarn through. Pull to tighten.

Chain (ch)

Place the yarn over the hook and pull through the loop (5).

Slip Stitch (sl st)

Insert the hook into the stitch, place the yarn over the hook, and pull through the stitch and loop on the hook (6).

Single Crochet (sc)

Insert the hook into the stitch, place the yarn over the hook, and pull through the stitch, so that two loops are on the hook (7). Place the yarn over the hook again and pull through both loops on the hook (8).

Half Double Crochet (hdc)

Place the yarn over the hook and insert the hook into the stitch (9). Yarn over and pull through the stitch. Place the yarn over the hook again and pull through all three loops on the hook (10).

Double Crochet (dc)

Place the yarn over the hook and insert the hook into the stitch (11). Yarn over and pull through the stitch, so that three loops are left on the hook (12). Yarn over and pull through the first two loops on the hook, so that two loops are left on the hook. Yarn over and pull through the remaining two loops.

Treble Crochet (tr)

Place the yarn over the hook twice and insert the hook into the stitch (13). Yarn over and pull through the stitch. Yarn over and pull through the first two loops on the hook, so that there are three loops left on the hook (14). Yarn over and pull through the first two loops on the hook again, so that there are two loops left on the hook. Yarn over again and pull through the remaining two loops.

1

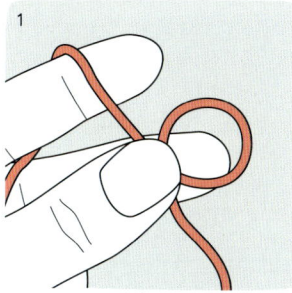

2

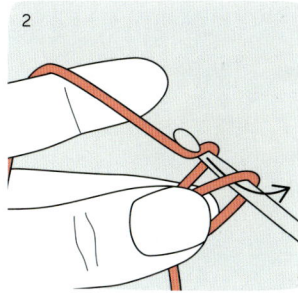

3

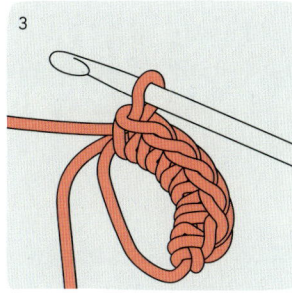

4

5

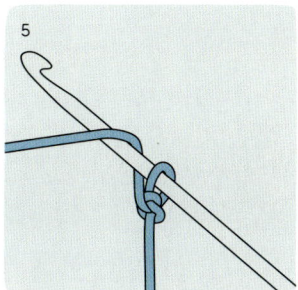

6

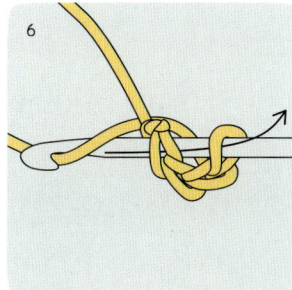

7

8

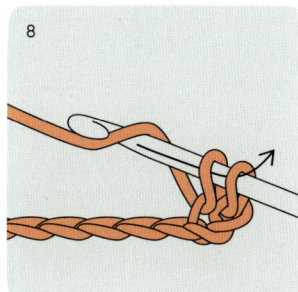

9

10

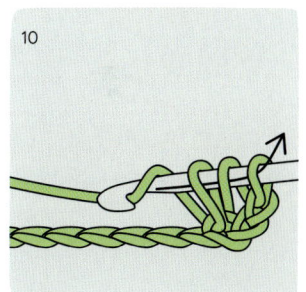

11

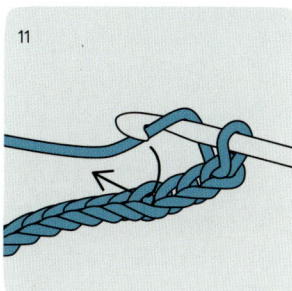

12

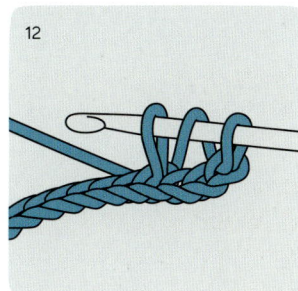

13

14

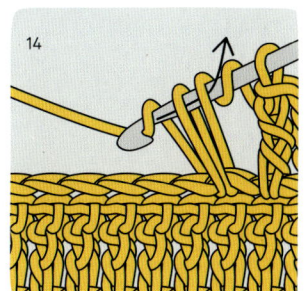

DECREASING STITCHES

Invisible Single Crochet Decrease

The standard method of decreasing can leave a small gap or bump when making a three-dimensional piece. Using the invisible single crochet decrease when making amigurumi results in a smoother and more even fabric.

Insert the hook into the front loop of the first stitch and then directly into the front loop of the second stitch, place the yarn over the hook (1), and draw the yarn through both of the front loops on your hook, two loops are now on the hook. Place the yarn over the hook again and draw the yarn through both loops on your hook to finish a single crochet stitch (2).

This also works for taller stitches such as hdc or dc decreases.

Standard Single Crochet Decrease (sc2tog)

Insert the hook into the first stitch, place the yarn over the hook, and pull a loop through the stitch, two loops are now on the hook (3). Insert the hook into the second stitch, place the yarn over the hook, and pull a loop through the stitch, three loops are now on the hook (4). Place the yarn over the hook and pull through all three loops on the hook.

Standard Half Double Crochet Decrease (hdc2tog)

Place the yarn over the hook and insert the hook into the first stitch (5). Place the yarn over again and pull a loop through the stitch, three loops are now on the hook (6). Insert the hook into the second stitch (7). Yarn over the hook and pull through the stitch, four loops are now on the hook (8). Yarn over and pull through all four loops on the hook.

Standard Double Crochet Decrease (dc2tog)

Place the yarn over the hook and insert the hook into the first stitch (9). Yarn over and pull a loop through the stitch, three loops are now on the hook (10). Yarn over and pull through the first two loops on the hook, two loops are now on the hook (11). Yarn over and insert the hook into the second stitch (12). Yarn over and pull through the stitch, four loops are now on the hook (13). Yarn over and pull through the first two loops on the hook, three loops are now on the hook (14). Yarn over and pull through all three loops on the hook.

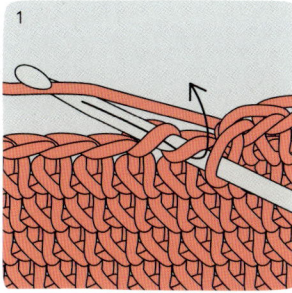

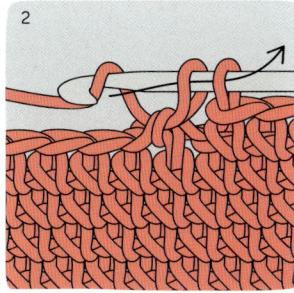

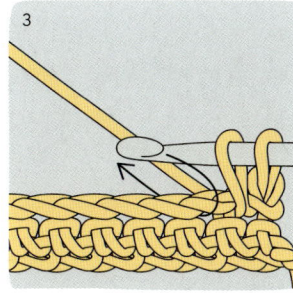

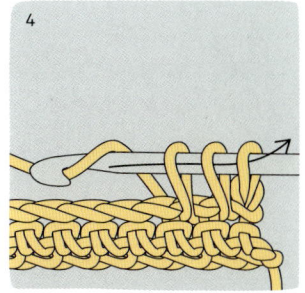

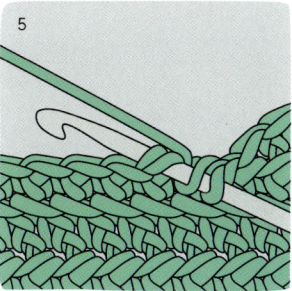

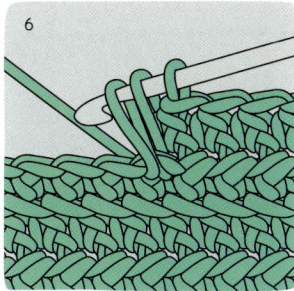

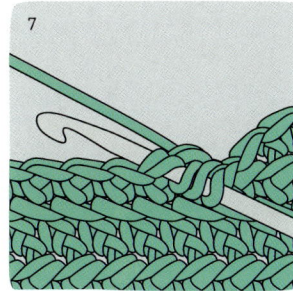

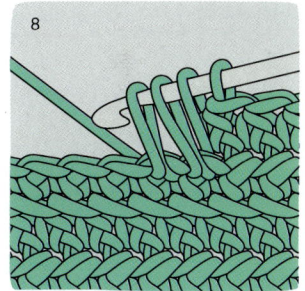

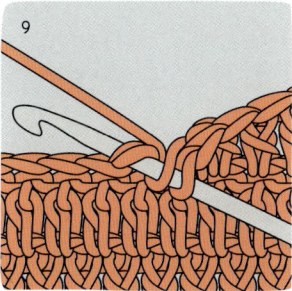

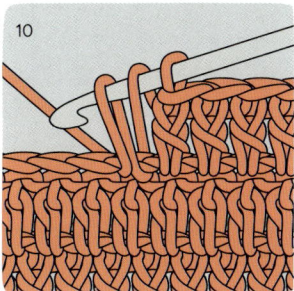

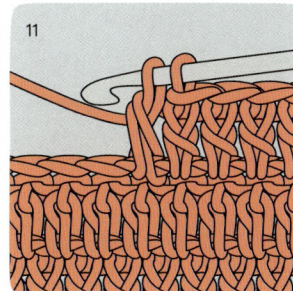

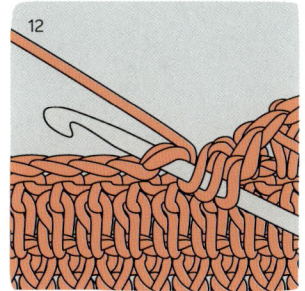

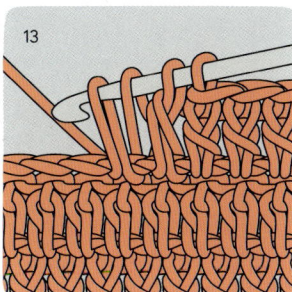

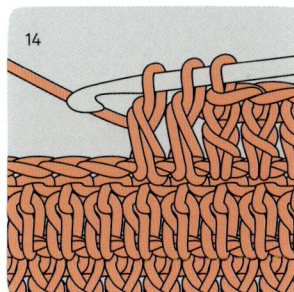

SPECIAL STITCHES

5-Double Crochet Bobble (5-dc-bl)

Place the yarn over the hook and insert the hook into the stitch, yarn over and pull the yarn through the stitch, yarn over and draw yarn through the first two loops on the hook, two loops are now on the hook.

Yarn over and insert hook into the same stitch. Yarn over and pull the yarn through the stitch. Yarn over and draw yarn through the first two loops on the hook, three loops are now on the hook.

Repeat the last step until you have six loops on the hook (1). Yarn over and pull the yarn through all six loops on the hook. Make a chain to secure the stitch (2).

3-Double Crochet Bobble (3-dc-bl)

This is worked in the same way as a 5-Double Crochet Bobble except that you only make a total of three double crochet stitches instead of five, so in the last step you will have four loops on the hook to pull the yarn through.

Chain-2 Picot (ch-2 picot)

Chain 2, slip stitch in 2nd ch from hook.

Chain-3 Picot (ch-3 picot)

Chain 3, slip stitch in 2nd ch from hook (3).

Front Post Half Double Crochet (fphdc)

Place the yarn over the hook and insert the hook from front to back around the post (the upright part) of the stitch (4). Yarn over and pull up a loop, three loops are now on the hook (5). Yarn over and pull the yarn through all three loops on the hook (6).

Right Side / Wrong Side of Crocheted Fabric

When crocheting in rounds it's important to be able to distinguish which side of the crocheted piece is the right side. This is especially true when you are asked to work in the front or back loops of a stitch.

On the right or front side there are little "V"s that appear (7). The wrong or back side has horizontal lines which are called back bumps or back bars (8).

Front Loop (FLO)

The front loop of a stitch is the loop closest to you. If the crochet pattern says to work in front loops only (FLO) you will work your stitches into just this front loop (9).

Back Loop (BLO)

The back loop is the loop furthest away from you. If the crochet pattern says to work in back loops only (BLO) you will work your stitches into just this back loop (10).

Back Bump / Back Bar

The back bump or back bar can be found on the "wrong side" of the fabric and lies right below the back loop of a stitch (11 and 12).

Back Bump / Back Bar of a Foundation Chain

On the front or right side of your crochet chain, the stitches are smooth and look like a series of interlocking "V"s (13). On the back or wrong side, the stitches are bumpy (14).

Crocheting in the back bumps along a chain creates a neater finish.

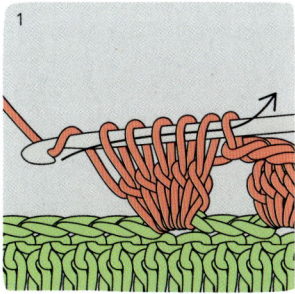

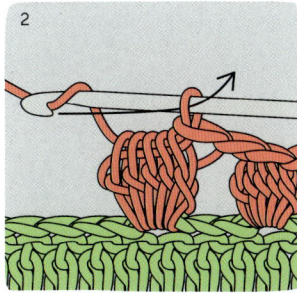

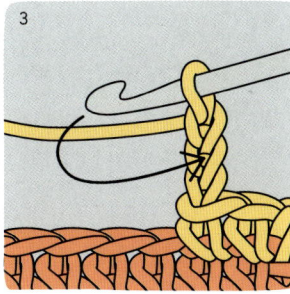

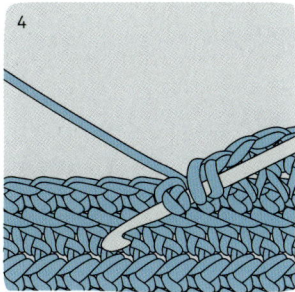

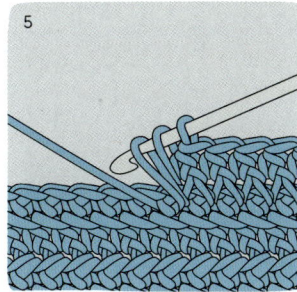

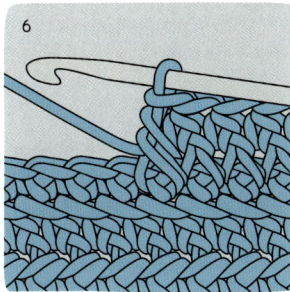

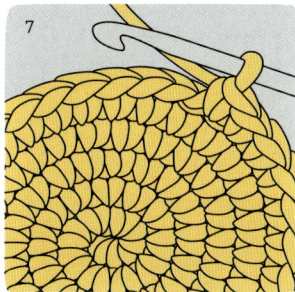

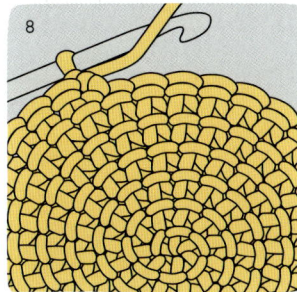

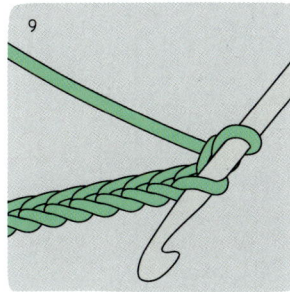

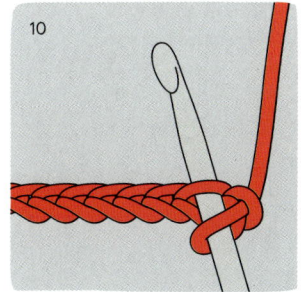

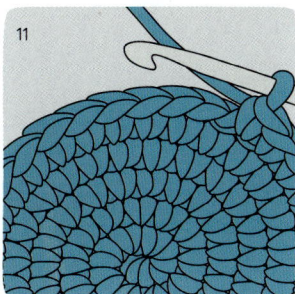

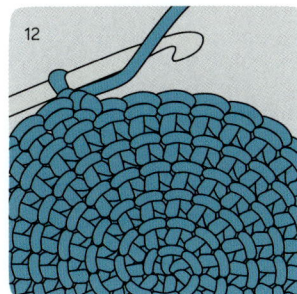

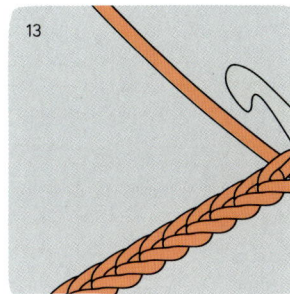

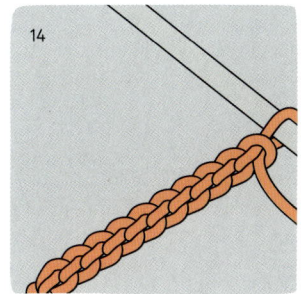

COLORWORK

Changing Colors

The color change method used throughout this book is to change the color in the last step of the previous stitch. Start the previous stitch as usual, but when completing the last yarn over pull through the new color (1). Drop the old yarn color and continue making the next stitch with the new color (2 and 3).

Joining Yarn

Insert the hook into the indicated stitch, wrap the yarn around the hook and pull it through the stitch, yarn over the hook, and pull through to secure (4).

Carrying Yarn / Crocheting With Two Colors

Carrying the yarn means you don't have to fasten the yarn off and rejoin a new strand each time you make a color change. This technique is helpful when making the Candy Cane pattern because a color change is made every few rounds.

There are various methods for doing this but carrying the yarn up at the beginning of each round is the technique used in this book. To do this, change the yarn color in the last step of the previous stitch (see Changing Colors) by simply letting the current color drop and by picking up the new color.

Keep the carried strand of yarn tight enough so that it lies flat against the wrong side of the fabric and doesn't catch on anything, but don't pull the strand too tight or the fabric will pucker.

FINISHING

Fasten Off

Cut the yarn and pull the yarn tail through the last loop on your hook.

Invisible Fasten Off

When you fasten off invisibly you get a smooth even edge. Cut the yarn and pull the yarn tail through the last stitch. Thread the yarn tail onto a yarn needle, insert the needle, from front to back, into the next stitch. Now insert the needle back into the same stitch that the yarn tail is coming out of, but into the back loop only, and pull gently (5). Weave the tail end into the wrong side of the fabric and cut the excess (6).

Weave In Ends As You Go

When changing colors with a three-dimensional piece, you can weave in the initial yarn tail of the new color and the remaining yarn tail of the previous color as you go by "carrying" both yarn tails. To do this, lay both yarn tails along the edge on top of the stitches to be worked and crochet over the strands for the next five to six stitches.

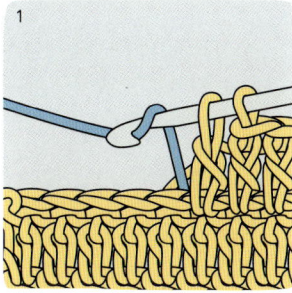

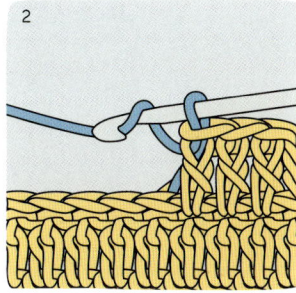

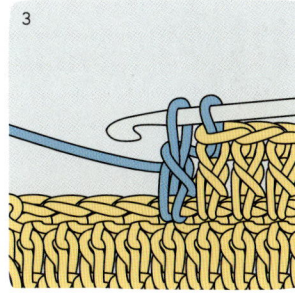

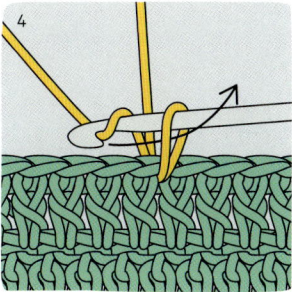

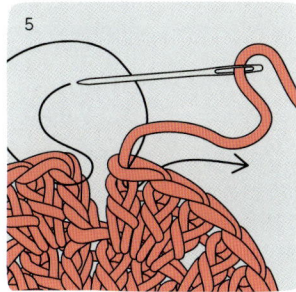

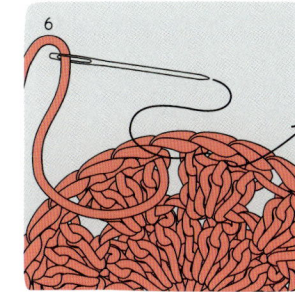

MAKING UP

Inserting Safety Eyes

Safety Note: Do not use toy safety eyes if giving to a child under three years of age. Instead, use black yarn to embroider the eyes.

Each pattern indicates which rows or rounds the safety eyes should be placed in and how many stitches there should be between them. Make sure you are happy with the placement of the safety eyes before pushing the washer onto the rod of the eye because once the washer is placed you won't be able to pull it off again.

Stuffing

Stuffing a piece firmly, but not so much that the stuffing shows between the stitches, is my secret to knowing how much fiberfill stuffing to use.

Closing Stitches Through Front Loops

Cut the yarn and pull the yarn tail through the last stitch. Thread onto a yarn needle. Insert the needle through the front loops only of each of the remaining stitches (1 and 2). Pull gently to close the hole (3). Insert the needle in the center of the stitches you just closed and come out in any direction from the middle of the crocheted piece (4). Tie a knot close to the amigurumi and push the knot inside the crocheted piece. Cut the excess yarn tail. The same technique applies when closing through the back loops only. You just insert your needle in the back loops instead.

Crocheting Two Pieces Together

Line up the stitches from both rounds that need to be crocheted together by placing one round of stitches on top of the other (5). With the yarn that has not been fastened off from one of the crochet pieces, single crochet around the entire piece working in both loops of both pieces to join them together (6).

The same technique applies when closing through the back loops. You will just be inserting your needle in the back loops instead of the front loops as described.

Shaping

Shaping makes it possible for these kawaii characters to stand up straight on a flat surface. The goal while shaping, unless otherwise instructed in a pattern, is to create an indentation at the bottom of the amigurumi, but none at the top.

Thread a tapestry needle with yarn matching the color of the crocheted piece, and begin shaping by inserting the needle from the center bottom of a crocheted piece to the center top (7 and 8). Take the needle back down from the center top to slightly off the center bottom (9 and 10). Take the needle back up from the center bottom to the center top (11). Pull to create an indentation in the bottom of the crocheted piece (12). There should be no indentation in the top (13). Take the needle back down the center from the top to the bottom. Secure the yarn with two or three knots and weave in the ends.

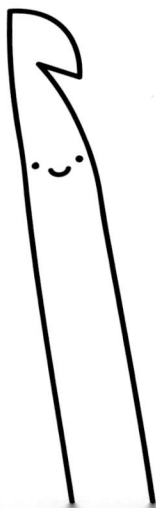

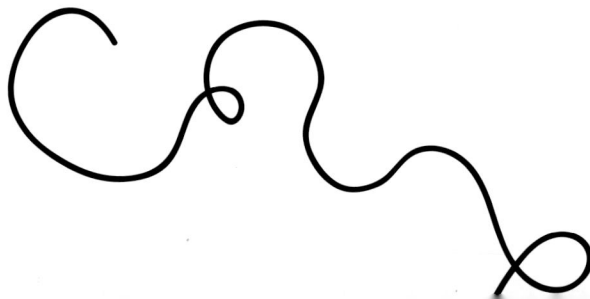

1

2

3

4

5

6

7

8

9

10

11

12

13

Ornament Hanging Loop

With needle and yarn, insert the needle through the top middle of the amigurumi piece (1). Insert the needle in the crochet fabric one stitch away and out of the crochet fabric where you previously exited (2). Pull yarn until the loop is the desired size (3). Tie a slip knot with the yarn tail and one end of the yarn loop (4). Insert needle next to the knot and out to the other side of the loop (5). Tie a slip knot with the yarn tail and end of the yarn loop (6). Insert needle next to the knot and out anywhere in the amigurumi piece (7).

With each yarn tail, tie a knot close to the amigurumi and push the knot inside the crocheted piece. Cut any excess yarn tail (8).

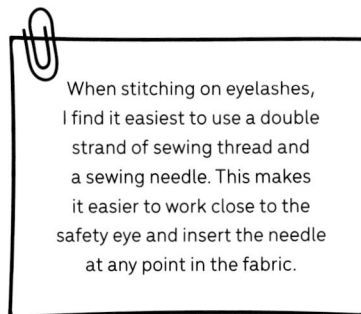

Fastening Off Inside a Three-Dimensional Piece

With the yarn tail threaded in a yarn needle, insert the needle through the entire middle of the crochet piece. Tie a knot close to the amigurumi and push the knot inside the crocheted piece. Cut any excess yarn tail.

Crocheting with Floral Wire

Cut wire to the length specified in the pattern. Hold the wire behind the foundation chain of stitches (9). Insert your hook into the chain stitch and under the wire. Crochet stitches as normal; doing so will cause the yarn to wrap around the wire as you crochet (10 and 11).

Stitching Facial Details

With **black** yarn, insert the yarn needle in the amigurumi at any point in the back and stitch on a "V" for the mouth. The mouth should be placed in the center between the eyes and almost the same height as the eyes, but one round down (12 and 13).

With the desired cheek color, insert the yarn needle in the amigurumi at any point in the back (14). Stitch on cheeks on either side of the eyes and almost the same width as the eyes, but one round down (15 and 16).

After stitching on both cheeks, insert the needle through the entire middle of the crochet piece. Tie a knot close to the amigurumi and push the knot inside the crocheted piece. Cut any excess yarn tail.

When stitching on eyelashes, I find it easiest to use a double strand of sewing thread and a sewing needle. This makes it easier to work close to the safety eye and insert the needle at any point in the fabric.

1

2

3

4

5

6
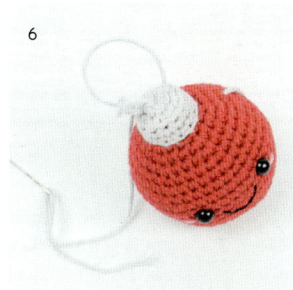

7

8

9
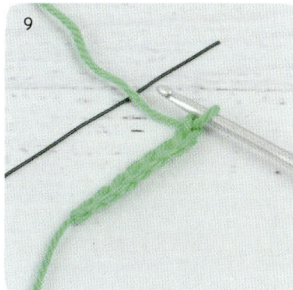

10

11
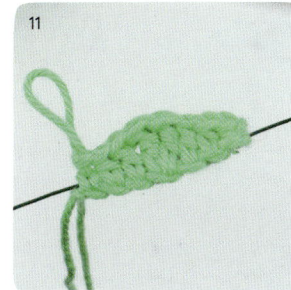

12

13

14

15

16

#kawaiicrochet

ABOUT THE AUTHOR

Melissa Bradley-Vatcher is a crochet designer and color enthusiast who has a love for all things handmade. She has a bachelor's degree in interior design and is a certified florist, but it was after the birth of her second child that she fell in love with a new medium of design: yarn. If she doesn't have a crochet hook in hand, she can be found baking or out in the garden. You can find her patterns on Etsy, Ravelry, and LoveCrochet. She lives in Utah, USA.

ACKNOWLEDGMENTS

I would like to express my sincere gratitude to my husband Michael, for his enthusiastic support and encouragement throughout the process of creating and publishing this book of crochet patterns. His love and belief in me have been my biggest motivation and has brought me so much joy.

Also, I would like to thank the lovely and talented team at David & Charles. Thank you, Ame Verso, for believing in me, yet again, and letting me be my best creative self. Thank you, Anna Wade, Jeni Chown, Lucy Ridley, Jason Jenkins, and Lindsay Kaubi for your dedication and hard work in bringing this project to life.

Last but not least, a special thank you to my children for inspiring me with their creativity and for being my little helpers during photoshoots and when I needed honest feedback. This book would not have been possible without the love and support of my family.

INDEX

A DAVID AND CHARLES BOOK
© David and Charles, Ltd 2025

David and Charles is an imprint of David and Charles, Ltd
Suite A, Tourism House, Pynes Hill, Exeter, EX2 5WS

A catalogue record for this book is available from the British Library.

ISBN-13: 9781446314425 paperback
ISBN-13: 9781446314432 EPUB

This book has been printed on paper from approved suppliers and made from pulp from sustainable sources.

FSC
www.fsc.org

MIX
Paper | Supporting
responsible forestry
FSC® C020056

Printed in China through Leo Paper Product Ltd. for:
David and Charles, Ltd
Suite A, Tourism House, Pynes Hill, Exeter, EX2 5WS

10 9 8 7 6 5 4 3 2 1

Publishing Director: Ame Verso
Publishing Manager: Jeni Chown
Project Editor: Lindsay Kaubi
Technical Editor: Sharon Carter
Lead Designer: Sam Staddon
Designer: Lucy Ridley
Pre-press Designer: Susan Reansbury
Illustrations: Lucy Ridley and Kuo Kang Chen
Art Direction: Prudence Rogers
Photography: Jason Jenkins
Production Manager: Beverley Richardson

David and Charles publishes high-quality books on a wide range of subjects. For more information visit www.davidandcharles.com.

Share your makes with us on social media using #dandcbooks and follow us on Facebook and Instagram by searching for @dandcbooks.

Layout of the digital edition of this book may vary depending on reader hardware and display settings.

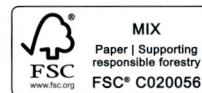